SELECTING
CHURCH
LEADERS

SELECTING CHURCH LEADERS

A Practice in
Spiritual Discernment

CHARLES M. OLSEN

ELLEN MORSETH

UPPER
ROOM BOOKS®
NASHVILLE

"The Second Giving" from *The Selected Poetry of Jessica Powers*, published by ICS Publications, Washington, D.C., 1991 Copyright by Carmelite Monastery, Pewaukee, WI. Used with permission.

The authors gratefully acknowledge all those who allowed the use of their "Witnesses" to illustrate the practice of spiritual discernment.

Cover Design: Uttley/DouPonce DesignWorks
Cover Art: Christ as Good Shepherd. Mosaic: Mausoleum of Galla Placidia, Ravenna, Italy/Scala/Art Resource, New York
The cover art is an ancient mosaic depicting sheep discerning the voice of their Shepherd.

Interior Design: Uttley/DouPonce DesignWorks
First Printing: 2002

Library of Congress Cataloging-in-Publication Data
Olsen, Charles M.
        Selecting church leaders : a practice in spiritual discernment / by Charles M. Olsen and Ellen Morseth.
        p. cm.
Includes bibliographical references (p.) and index.
ISBN 0-8358-0961-7
        1. Church officers. 2. Christian leadership. 3. Discernment of spirits. I. Morseth, Ellen, 1942- II. Title.
BV705 .046 2002
253--dc21   2001045380

Printed in the United States of America

*This book is dedicated to all
who are exploring the role of the "Spirit" and the "us"
in the selection of church leadership,
especially our extended family
of Worshipful-Work colleagues and friends.*

CONTENTS

PREFACE

So you find yourself in the selector's seat. Welcome to the club! You are not the first and won't be the last. Persons before you have experienced the ecstasy and agony of selecting leaders for every level of church life. For some it has been a rewarding, satisfying, or even inspiring experience. Some report that it has been life-changing! Others say, "Never again." Beyond accomplishing a necessary task— filling slots for the church's management grid— those who don't want to repeat the experience received little personal reward for their investment of time and energy. They even may have come away from the experience worn out, burned out, and disillusioned. Perhaps, after the leader was selected, they became their selectee's severest critics. In the most extreme cases, they may have left the church. Their expectations had not been met, and their energy and hope had been so depleted that the exit door seemed like the only viable option.

You may be in the selector's seat as a member of the congregation's nominating committee with the duty of looking for committed, able, and effective leaders for the church's boards, committees, organizations, or ministry teams. You may be in that seat to find persons to replace yourself as a leader in an organization within the congregation. You may find yourself on a pastor search committee, charged with the important task of selecting a new pastor who will provide leadership for a good span of years to come. You may be part of a committee or board faced with the challenge of selecting its own chairperson from its membership. Your judicatory, diocese, district, or conference may have tapped you to appoint lay- or clergypersons who can guide the church at a particular level of the system. Or you may have the high privilege of helping to nominate or select an executive, bishop, or the spiritual head of your larger faith community!

When you slip with others into selectors' seats, you will face dilemmas immediately. Will you try to "get the job over with" as quickly as you can? Or will you be patient and allow the process to run its course and take as long as that process dictates? Will you try to come to agreement with as much ease as possible—trading elementary compromises in order to move to closure? Or will you probe as deep as you can for as long as necessary—even if the process produces conflict and puts your companion members at odds with one another's values and preferences?

Will you seek to satisfy the immediate and obvious needs of the organization with your choice? Or will you engage patiently in the process of coming to a shared vision of the faith community's long-term needs and opportunities? Will you automatically fill the leadership slots on the church's organizational chart? Or will you ask hard questions about what structure the church actually needs to accomplish its ministry in accord with God's call and leading?

Once you have closed on a selection, will you put a "hard sell" on the chosen person to convince the selectee of the selectors' wisdom? Or will you engage the selectee in a thorough exploration of her or his gifts and calling for this expression of ministry?

Welcome to the seat. We offer you what wisdom we have gathered around the deep and long-standing practice of spiritual discernment. We pray that your ride in this seat will be one that is blessed by God, beneficial in your own faith formation, and useful in the selection of persons to serve God in new and exciting ways.

INTRODUCTION

"Your Ways" and "My Ways"

The great council meeting in Jerusalem recorded in the fifteenth chapter of the Book of Acts resolved a huge and thorny issue that had faced the infant church. Would gentile converts to Christianity be required to participate in Jewish rituals in order to be part of the new community? The followers of Jesus had an opportunity to engage in discernment under the guidance of the Spirit, while remembering Jesus' teaching and recalling his manner of life.

Even with the tradition and the law lying alongside the witness of Jesus, the body of Christ was faced with living into and out of Jesus' promise to send the Spirit, who would lead them into all truth. The new church would need to enter into discernment of the mind of Christ through the witness of the Spirit. In other words, the church had to discern the mind of Christ in the specific context in which the people lived.

When the church gathered in Jerusalem, the people told stories about the signs and wonders of the Spirit's work among them. They cited the scriptures, noting where their own experience dovetailed with the tradition. They prayed and submitted themselves to one another and to the leading of the Spirit. They debated with sharp minds and tongues. They listened to the wisdom of sages like James, leader of the mother church in Jerusalem. Compassionately they tuned their hearts to the people who would be affected by their decision. The eventual decision of the apostles and elders was affirmed by the whole church.

When all was said and done, the Jerusalem elders and apostles crafted a letter to the church in Antioch, informing that church of their decision and offering guidance for ordering common life together at Antioch. By unanimous decision, the Jerusalem church sent the letter by the hand of trusted servants who could personalize the information and offer pastoral interpretation and support. In that famous letter a clause jumps off the page: "It has seemed good to the Holy Spirit and to us." What a statement! Its implication is profound, mystical, sensible, and suggests the strange twists that the Spirit so often introduces into our lives.

"It has seemed good to the Holy Spirit." God is not distant from the decision. The living spirit of Jesus fulfills the great prayer for the unity of the church in John 17. God entrusts decision making to humans who can use all the faculties that God imparts. How the two—God and human—come together is a mystery, a matter with which theologians can wrestle. But for our purpose in this book, we will claim both converging roads—the Spirit's and ours.

So often these two roads run at a distance from one another without regard or reference to each other. Sometimes these roads cross or collide. God's ways are not always our ways and vice versa.

> For my thoughts are not your thoughts,
>> nor are your ways my ways, says the Lord (Isa. 55:8).

When we say, "Forget all that religious stuff; let's just use our best judgment and decide what we think suits our needs and situation," we fulfill the scripture in Isaiah. Sometimes we do not recognize what God is up to and what God would speak. Our eyes are not focused and our ears are not tuned to God's wavelength. God may broadcast beyond what our receivers can hear.

Suppose we turned our sentences around to read from right to left, as Hebrew scriptures are read. Our programmed way of reading from left to right might blind us from seeing the message:

> For my thoughts are not your thoughts,
> nor are your ways my ways, says the Lord

In spiritual discernment we seek to bring God's ways and our ways into congruence. Seeming good to the Spirit *and* seeming good to us come together after a patient, prayerful process and faithful engagement in a set of practices. We will want to embrace those spiritual practices that open us to the mystery and presence of God: attending to the witness of scripture, quieting ourselves in solitude and silence, relinquishing ego and the need to prevail, and offering ourselves in worship.

"It has seemed good to . . . us." We will boldly claim and exercise all of those good gifts with which God has endowed us in our creation. We will use those rational and analytical capacities that help us weigh and compare. We will honor those who come to and express wisdom by hunch and intuition. We will invite the grace of imagination from those who see reality via pictures. We will listen to the narratives of our sisters and brothers who bring both current and ancient stories to bear on current topics. We will sit together and alone in solitude to allow latent wisdom to surface and find voice in few words. Discernment in selection of church leaders allows us to claim our human identity and gifts as useful tools with which to gain insight into God's will and leading. Both the "Spirit" and the "us" are vitally important. Claim both and be prepared to live into the mystery and high calling of selecting church leaders.

In the chapters that follow we will introduce you to stories from the witness of scripture about the selection of leaders. The process of selection and the dynamics that selectors experience are described from the vantage point of the selectees. These first-person narratives follow the biblical record, with liberties taken only to emphasize both the subtle and obvious intricacies of the text.

Other stories from congregational and church-system contexts will illustrate models of selection where participants followed an intentional spiritual discernment process or stumbled upon one. We pray that this book will produce a new generation of stories about how the selection of church leaders has been accomplished with the alchemy of the "Spirit" and the "us"!

1

WHOSE CHOICE:
GOD'S OR OURS?

God,
Show us
Whom you are selecting
At this time
To lead this church!

God, Whom Are You Selecting?

How we frame the question for discernment makes all the difference in the world. Chapter 4 of *Discerning God's Will Together*, which serves as a companion book to this one, presents ten *movements* that chart the waters of spiritual discernment. These movements are drawn from the historic experience of various faith communities that have developed practices and procedures for communal decision making. Picture the movements as stepping-stones on the surface of a reflection pond. We may or may not follow a predetermined sequence in crossing the pond. But having the stepping-stones positioned before us with names and meanings of their supportive nature provides the discerners with options from which to choose. One stone is "framing."

However the other nine stepping-stones are arranged or used, position the one called "framing" near the edge as a starting place. How will we frame our question for discerning church leaders: Whom do *we* think should be selected for leadership, or whom is *God* selecting for leadership? We can frame the matter for discernment either from our viewpoint or from God's viewpoint. One church board member reported the difference that a reframed question made when board members moved from doing church business "the American way" out of their own wisdom to asking, "What is the mind of Christ in this matter?" That simple shift changed the focus. The board no longer did business as usual. The members refocused to do God's business.

Are we willing to ask the "God" question—that is, placing our decision in the light and framework of God's agenda and view of reality? In practicing this process of prayerful discernment, beginning a question with the name of God or addressing God initially helps clarify the real question. This practice puts the question in proper perspective.

Even though we all are vitally involved in the selection process, we are in it to live out the Lord's Prayer petition "your will be done, on earth" (Matt. 6:10). God, who? when? where? how? When we get these questions straight up front, we can focus our striving and energy on a purpose beyond ourselves rather than against one another or in several different directions.

For the generic purpose of this chapter, the question before us could be framed thusly: "God, whom are you selecting/calling at this time to lead in this church? Show us your choice." We are invited to participate in God's own choice.

Show Us

Who are the "we" engaged in the selection process? In most church settings, the selection is made in a communal setting—that is, by a group of people. In some situations an individual may have the authority or permission to make a selection. But even then, such a designated person usually consults with others and listens to advice. Hierarchical systems most often employ a communal process. The abbot of one Benedictine monastery reported: "I do not make independent decisions here. The community engages in a process of discernment, and then I name and formalize the decision."

Nominating committees, search groups, and selection teams all require an intentional and open process of interaction among their members. To be invited into a selection process carries with it the secondary, perhaps the primary, invitation into life in community. As such, the invitation also calls for conversion and formation. Folks simply do not come out of a selection experience as the same persons who entered. In his book *Life Together,* Dietrich Bonhoeffer likens the invitation into community as an invitation to die to the community's own wishes and dreams! Self-death, self-discovery, and self-empowerment all temper and forge the character of the selectees. Persons who have served one or more years on a pastor search committee often describe the experience as life-changing and faith-forming. They say they come away from that time not only with a new, deeper understanding of the theology and polity of the church or the nuances of leadership but as different persons.

So prepare to be changed. If the process only follows a culturally conditioned "let's do what we think is best" script, you may be able to complete the task with little personal mark to show for it (unless it is a scar!). On the other hand, if an intentional, prayerful, and patient process of discernment is undertaken, then the core of one's identity, character, and faith will be altered, deepened, and elevated!

The selection group will take on a life of its own. Like a baby, it will be conceived, grow, experience birth and growth pains, function, and eventually terminate. Along that timeline a story will emerge and develop. The group will create its own language and symbols, discover its own humor and wisdom, and find signs and signals of God's presence along the way. This journey is an adventure. No two groups will ever be the same, even though they may operate within the same familiar denominational structure. A new community is to be birthed by the Spirit. Count on it. Grow in it. And celebrate this community as a gift from God!

In the selection and subsequent anointing of David, the "us" consisted secondarily of a father, neighbors, community elders, siblings, and primarily a prophet, Samuel. They all had something to learn in the experience, for events certainly took some strange twists! They had to see through new eyes to see God's way of being part of the selection process.

A BIBLICAL WITNESS

from David, a Selectee
(based on 1 Samuel 16)

Folks always said I had a big heart—even a sincere heart. And some even said they imagined it was like the heart of God. Those observations shocked me. I saw myself as a simple lad who minded my own business. I was aware of God's presence and sensed that the hand of God was upon me, even though I did not know where God's direction might lead.

I was surprised, but perhaps not completely, by the events on the day when the famous prophet Samuel came to our village. In a whirl of excitement, suddenly I was anointed as king to replace Saul! Talk about a shift in identity. Caring for sheep was one thing—but a nation? I did not think I was capable.

So for days on end I talked with the elders, my father, and my brothers to try to understand God's purpose. What had gone through Samuel's mind as he tried to discern where God was in this dramatic change?

I learned that Samuel had had it "up to here" with Saul. Samuel had been stampeded into anointing Saul earlier because the people had demanded a king. Samuel knew their cry was a rejection of God, but he finally anointed a king to satisfy their demand and because the Lord had said to listen to them. Saul had looked promising. He was tall, athletic, and decisive. Over the years, though, Samuel saw that Saul's kingship was not working. Driven to his wit's end, he heard the voice of God from deep inside saying, "Stop your grieving. It's time to move on."

Samuel was prompted to seek out my father, Jesse, in Bethlehem, sensing that a good prospect for king could come from among his many sons. Samuel did not come ill-prepared. Very deliberately he prepared himself spiritually for the trip. His intent to offer sacrifice served as a "cover" for his journey for Saul, but the sacrifice signified also the importance of an act of worship into which he would invite the elders and my family. The sacrifice would cost an expensive heifer, but it also would signal relinquishment, letting go and trusting God for direction. Samuel had no idea of his final decision. He only knew that he would begin with worship and then God would show him what to do.

In that setting of worship Samuel offered a gesture—no, more than a gesture—an act of sanctifying the worshiping community. Samuel, my family, and the elders were on holy ground, part of a holy ritual, and contemplating a holy selection to be conducted with holy hands. They were all in the hands of God.

At the appropriate moment, Samuel called for my eldest brother, Eliab. He seemed like a shoo-in—the eldest with rights of authority and inheritance. The firstborn was always holy to the Lord and dedicated to God's use, right? Eliab was Samuel's first inclination, but Samuel had no peace about this potential selection. Words kept surfacing from his heart: "Do not look on his appearance or on the height of his stature, because I have rejected him." (It must have been the voice of the Lord.) "The Lord does not see as mortals see; they look on the outward appearance, but the Lord looks on the heart" [1 Sam. 16:7]. You can imagine the shock of the elders who served on this selection committee. When these words were repeated like a mantra as each of my seven brothers passed before him, even the elders were beginning to get the point!

Then Samuel asked if there was anyone else. By this time he must have wondered whether God was in this process or not. "Only the youngest and least likely. He is out tending the sheep," replied my father. Samuel asked for me, overcoming his doubt and fear by continuing the search process under the hope that this trip was not to be in vain. When he saw my ruddy appearance, he came up close and looked into my eyes for the longest time. It was as if he were peering into the window of my heart. Neither one of us spoke. Now the inner voice sent a different message: "Rise and anoint him; for this is the one" (v. 12). Then he proceeded to anoint me while my brothers gathered around. Everyone seemed to be involved. God seemed to have used each one in a special way within the process.

As I have lived with and reflected upon this significant day, I realize that God was doing the choosing. Samuel had consolation, an inner peace and assurance. The elders recognized his choice. And miracle of miracles—even my brothers gathered and celebrated with me in the anointing and

by eating with me at the feast, as was the custom at a sacrifice.
And Dad? He was very proud!

❖

A selection group—the "we"—becomes a covenant community. Early on in its life a group's members will do well to create explicit covenants. Operating on an implicit covenant eventually will result in some form of impasse. The group will break down in conflict, wander in uncertainty, climb all over one another, and take an exorbitant amount of time dealing with internal matters. Establishing a clear covenant empowers each person in the group.

This covenant will address such matters as confidentiality, honesty, attentiveness, attendance, and specific commitments. But if it is to foster God's selection, then a covenant will include a commitment to a patient and prayerful process of spiritual discernment. Framing a matter for discernment invites that commitment. Many of the movements, stepping-stones, presented in this book will become essential elements of a covenant to discern. Participants will covenant to seek the mind of Christ. They will seek to know and express God's will/yearning, join in prayer, listen deeply to one another and to the Spirit, relinquish ego dominance with its need to prevail, engage the scriptures, and reflect on the historic witness of their own faith community.

The covenant will honor what each person brings. One small-group member, when asked what was most significant about life in that little faith community, replied, "Here we have learned to celebrate the uniqueness of one another!" Sister Mary Benet McKinney, whose writing and teaching have invited the church to recall the ancient tradition of wise discretion and discernment, says that everyone has "a piece of the wisdom."[1] Each person is to be celebrated. Each person's story will be respected and drawn upon. Each person's gifts will be valued. Yes, and each person's idiosyncrasies will be tolerated!

When new groups form for specific tasks, the participants often share their own faith stories. Since we are forming community around leadership selection, one or more of the following questions or statements may prime the proverbial pump.

- Describe a person who was influential in your faith formation.
- Relate a "moment" from a deliberative group experience when you were moved in a particular way, whether to laughter, tears, insight, discomfort, inspiration, or other feeling.
- Describe an experience in selecting a leader for a group that turned out well or not so well or disastrously!
- Detail your own considerations in a decision to say yes or no to an invitation to leadership.
- Relate how a decision-making process in which you were a participant took a "strange twist."
- Describe how you have seen God present in the work of a deliberative group.

The time you take to share faith stories will not be wasted. In fact, we often see that in addition to forming community and connecting people with common and divergent experiences, those stories become touchstones and wells of wisdom that people will draw upon later in the process.

In the early stages of group formation, folks often discover, name, and celebrate the similarities in their stories and how much they have in common. But as community deepens they also will uncover a new reality: "We are very different! We even annoy one another and get under one another's skin!" With this disappointment and disillusionment, the group has the opportunity to recognize that the basis of its life together is not personal affinity but the grace of God. Moving into that acceptance will free group members to engage in their work together. Ultimately the grace of God rather than their affinity with one another will be the glue that holds them together.

The process of uncovering possible friction points may be anticipated early on with an invitation to share "what you can look for in me" and "what you need to look out for in me." Several good resources are available to assist the group in appreciating the learning style and operating preferences of each participant. Since the discernment process is spiritually rooted, we commend Corinne Ware's book *Discover Your Spiritual Type* and the instrument she developed in that book (see Resources). Ware describes four distinct preferences in the way an individual orients her or his spiritual life. No one type holds a higher value than another. Understanding these variations creates a community of equals and affirms what all persons bring from their own faith journey. In addition to benefiting the group as a whole, this knowledge empowers each individual to be bold.

Other instruments, such as the widely used Myers-Briggs Type Indicator Personality Inventory, the Enneagram, or gifts-identification resources may help promote mutual respect within a group. Keep the emphasis on aspects of one's faith journey and attending to God's presence. One risk of using the profiles is becoming detached from one's faith journey and focusing on sociological, psychological, or professional coding apart from faith roots.

Richard A. Busch, in an article titled "A Strange Silence" published in the *Christian Century*, reports on his experience with pastors who attend continuing-education events at Episcopal Theological

Seminary in Alexandria, Virginia. When the pastors first arrive, they are invited to introduce themselves to others in the group. The pastors are more likely to express their identity in the language of Myers-Briggs than in that of faith journey. When they use Myers-Briggs terminology, everyone nods in understanding. Then, after several days of introduction to spiritual formation, they are asked again to present their own faith stories to one another, "with special attention to how they understand God to have been acting in their lives over the years." Busch says, "The goal of the assignment—to share how God has been acting in their lives—is not always realized. Traditional Christian language is rarely woven into the narrative. At least 80 percent of the personal stories do not integrate the individual's life with the Christian faith. The vocabulary has a professional, ecclesiastical or psychological flavor. . . . Many fail to notice what is missing." Why the "strange silence"? He continues, "I suspect . . . that behind this silence is finally this: the gospel is not the center of our lives, and our spiritual life is disconnected from the things that interest, worry and excite us."[2]

If professional clergy are not comfortable with articulating their own faith experience relative to God's presence, is it any wonder that laypersons are reticent? A model of avoidance may have been unwittingly showcased. The invitation to a selection group to form a common life by sharing faith stories may seem like raising the bar to be cleared, but the effort is worthwhile.

As the group forms, it will be important to develop a level playing field on which all participants share equal power. How can that happen, you ask, if a pastor or administrator bearing the authority of a leadership position sits with the group as either a participating or ex officio member? Establish a clear understanding early on in the group's formation. We have seen several working models to consider.

In one instance, the pastor is invited to participate at the formation stage when the selection tasks and boundaries are being established and when qualifications of potential selectees are outlined. Then the pastor leaves and allows the selecting group to do its work, returning only if and when the group seeks consultation. That policy empowers the group to do its work.

At times we have seen groups rely on and trust any confidential knowledge the pastor may have. This does not mean that the pastor brings a slate to the search group. If the committee has invited the congregation to suggest names for consideration, the pastor may feed names to the committee anonymously along with the members of the congregation. That way the names that emerge do not come with the pastor's recommendation attached.

Here is another possibility for a working relationship between a pastor and a nominating committee: If the pastor knows something about a potential selectee that could affect that person's ability to serve, she or he could feel free to say of that candidate, "I don't think this person's serving at this time would be a good idea." These exact words should be used only with the understanding that the committee will not request further elaboration. The kind of confidential information that could trigger that response might be the knowledge of a serious health crisis, impending marital breakup, difficulty with addiction, serious moral lapse, or the prospect of imminent relocation. Most committees appreciate and respect this covenant, although they are free to override it if they choose. As a matter of practice, it is rarely required and used.

When the selecting group is searching for a professional member of a church or judicatory staff, the senior pastor or administrator is also seeking a colleague. Other staff members will also welcome a colleague. In those situations the senior pastor or administrator plays a unique and critical role. He or she cannot dominate the process, rendering the committee an advisory group only. Neither can she or he be removed from or distanced from the process. In that situation it may be helpful to agree to a covenant of consensus for closing on a selectee. This agreement would provide the pastor with the opportunity to veto a candidate, but it also would provide the same opportunity to every other member of the group.

Identifying a person to exercise internal leadership becomes a final and critical decision for the group. What specific tasks of record keeping, communications, research, coordinating, and presiding over meetings need to be assigned? These decisions are tasks of discernment. Naming a chairperson or moderator for the group will test and tax the capacity of the group to engage in spiritual discernment. Who is God calling to serve in this leadership role within our group? The process of discernment, which is presented in this book, can map a way to make this important early decision. In fact, it will become an opportunity to practice discernment and then reflect on how it went!

At This Time

The times at which communities select leaders vary according to an annual ministry rhythm or current situation or opportunity. Framing a selection matter for discernment always involves a consideration of the context in which the leadership is needed, including the critical element of time. What time is it in the life of the organization?

Most congregational or judicatory leadership selections follow the rhythm of the annual church calendar. An annual meeting dictated for the legally incorporated nonprofit organization may trigger the selection process. The beginning of the program year, associated with "rally day" by some and coinciding with the beginning of the school year, signals the need for teachers and program leaders. Usually selection teams start their work several months or even a year in advance of an election or appointment date.

The rotation system, in which lay leadership is rotated on and off church boards and committees after a specific term (usually three years), was created to empower the laity. But in fact the revolving door has placed power in the hands of the clergy, for they are the only ones who stay on the boards and committees, thereby understanding the subtleties of how the groups operate. As time goes by, institutional memory may be lost. There is so much coming and going that a solid working group of leaders hardly has a chance to function together. Many who have experienced this system say that about the time they get the hang of one group's job and style, their term is up! Others realize that every time new persons are added to a body, even though they may constitute only one-quarter to one-third of the total membership, in reality a new board is created.

In our work with congregational leadership, we are aware of the enormous amount of energy that goes into the annual selection process. Nominating groups work long and hard. Often they become discouraged over the number of no-thank-you responses they receive. Training and preparation opportunities become shortchanged when pastors are stretched—already having more on their plate than they can handle. Sometimes there may be too few new officers or leaders to warrant a preparation "class," so people just slip in with no orientation. Once new people are in place on a board or committee, another round of organizational shuffle takes place as new committee chairs are chosen. All of this activity costs time and energy for the internal operation of the church, its mission beyond the church, and for individuals' family commitments. We wonder, *isn't there a better way?*

Here is one suggestion: Instead of searching for, electing, appointing, preparing, and organizing new leader groups every year to serve a three-year rotation system, why not go through the process only once every three years? That change would save energy spent in rotation and provide a designated group the time to work together cohesively. Most churches allow folks to serve two consecutive terms, so potentially individuals could serve for six years. This kind of system would also allow a selection group to work unhurried for up to a year to find a new cadre of leaders for the next three-year period.

Since the institution of parish pastoral councils by Vatican II is a relatively new kid on the ecclesiastical block, few rules and procedures have grown up around them. Roman Catholic parishes therefore have the freedom to put new parish pastoral councils in place according to their own internal rhythm. Typically these councils engage in an extensive discernment selection process, then leave the new council in place until the community discerns that it is time to repeat the process, anywhere from three to eight years!

Kennon Callahan observes in *Effective Church Leadership* that the rotation system is a mechanical one and often rotates people out of leadership positions before they become effective. Allowing persons to serve as long as they feel called and are validated by the community could improve their effectiveness.

Completion of tasks and fulfillment of current leaders' callings may signal a time to select new leaders. Our own organization, Worshipful-Work Center for Transforming Religious Leadership, has roots in a Lilly Endowment–funded project on the development of church boards and councils. Initially an advisory panel was assembled to provide direction. At the conclusion of that panel's task, several members became "discerning overseers" for the new ministry. After several years, when the ministry became incorporated as an ecumenical nonprofit organization, that team became its official board. Recently some members have moved off the board, feeling that they have completed their own sense of calling to birth and nurture a new organization. They have no less enthusiasm for the ministry, but they sense that it is time for new leadership and the move to a national rather than a regional board. These leaders are prepared to pass the baton. No calendar dictated the timing; rather, the internal development of the organization did. The organization's bylaws state that board membership be considered in a comprehensive way periodically—at least every three years, recognizing that the organization has a developmental clock with its own phases, stages, and rhythms. Often board members have this inner sense that "it's time."

Unique opportunities lying before the church or religious organization may dictate timing for a leadership search. When a congregation faces a capital campaign related to locating, relocating, renovating, or expanding facilities, or securing an endowment, it may need special new leadership. A new group of leaders may be in order for unique program or mission opportunities, such as, developing a small-group ministry; designing a lay academy; starting a caregiving program, day care facility, or children's school; restructuring the worship and music. Specialized ministries like these often call for leaders who have gifts and experience in these arenas.

Filling a pastoral vacancy is an obvious trigger for a selection process. A pastor may have resigned, been removed, or retired. The vacancy or approaching vacancy releases a new volume of energy— in terms of both hopes and fears among the congregation. Often lay leadership emerges during a pastoral vacancy, so the church needs to find a way to permit and invite individuals with new gifts to step forward during this transition period. A specialist in interim ministries and planning assistance from the larger judicatories can jumpstart the pastoral selection process. Welcome the assistance if this is your congregation's situation. The experience mined from a variety of scenarios by people at judicatory levels provides a wealth of understanding about the opportunities for development in a church during a pastoral vacancy. If the former pastor departed in an atmosphere of conflict or if the congregation finds itself in conflict, during the vacancy, specialists skilled in ministering within this atmosphere will help manifest the grace of God.

Consider timing as a gift from God. God is out to create something new in this faith community. The community moves to tiptoe when the aroma of selection fills the air.

For Samuel the time to select came when it was obvious to him and to others that Saul's leadership was not working. It was time to move on and take decisive action. "Samuel grieved over Saul. And the Lord was sorry that he had made Saul king over Israel. The Lord said to Samuel, 'How long will you grieve over Saul? I have rejected him from being king over Israel. Fill your horn with oil and set out; I will send you to Jesse the Bethlehemite, for I have provided for myself a king among his sons'" (1 Sam. 15:35–16:1).

Mary of Nazareth may not have realized the time was ripe when she was selected to be the mother of Jesus, but in the fullness of time God sent forth his Son born of a woman.

A BIBLICAL WITNESS
from Mary of Nazareth, a Selectee
(based on Luke 1:26-55; John 2:1-11; Acts 1:14)

I once had an extraordinary visit with an angel. You probably know the story. One afternoon the angel Gabriel told me that I was highly favored by God and had been chosen to give birth to Jesus, God's Son. I was at first frightened and skeptical. But then I heard that "nothing will be impossible with God" [Luke 1:37]. And that is true! I gave birth to Jesus, and Elizabeth, who was too old to become pregnant, conceived a son!

Today, years later, I'm not a distinguished person or royal figure as some folks would make me out to be. Ever since my visit from God's angel, I've been walking in the obscurity and mystery of life as much as you have. You could call me an unlettered, ordinary woman who has never held a leadership position among the faithful but a woman whose son has led her to some rich discoveries about leadership.

For thirty-plus years as an admiring parent I watched Jesus grow in wisdom and grace. Because of him I also experienced traumatic moments during those years, some like many parents go through—such as losing a child in a crowded setting. But always I have been aware of being favored by God, graced by learnings my son taught me, and blessed by what God has been able to do through my presence in the community.

One incident worth telling you occurred at a wedding feast in Cana. Jesus and I both attended. The ceremony and the subsequent festive banquet proceeded happily until I happened to notice that the wine was running short. I decided to draw my son's attention to this circumstance, even though I wasn't the host of the party. I just took the initiative to forestall an unpleasant situation. After our brief conversation, which somewhat puzzled me at the time, I directed the waiters to do whatever my son told them to do. Jesus asked the waiters to fill some empty jars with water. Naturally they were puzzled, but they did what they were asked to do, and the jars became full of the finest wine. Wow! This was the first miracle his friends and disciples ever witnessed, so the wedding party became even merrier!

But back to that puzzling conversation my son and I had just before this incident. Jesus matter-of-factly said to me, "My hour has not yet come." I did not understand then that his words referred to the hour of his impending death on the cross.

As you know, my son was an equalizer. His "last shall be first" proclamations threatened the political and religious order. His high regard for the dignity of women, for peace on earth, and for love among peoples wasn't always accepted in our culture. So my dear son—a spiritual leader recognized by some—was given an unfair trial and put to death.

The death of one's own innocent child is surely a mother's worst nightmare. I grieved inconsolably, but by the grace of God I was determined to continue the struggle Jesus had led for what is good and right and decent in this world.

After Jesus' resurrection I still wanted to be part of a community intentionally formed to spread my son's ideals. Deciding to be present in the upstairs room in Jerusalem where his followers gathered to pray was easy for me. The people who came together there, and elsewhere since, validate my call to leadership by including me in their company and giving testimony to the graces with which God continues to gift me.

I continue trying to inspire society's less fortunate folks to look for the right time and to aim toward their fair share in leadership opportunities and decision-making possibilities and responsibilities.

Since the timely visit of an angel and throughout all my life, my spirit continues to find joy in God. I know that I am highly favored by God. And I know too that every person must follow his or her call, count on God's generous graces, and live within the support of a community.

Historians have made much of the context for the coming of Christ, an era of peaceful stability, good roads, access to travel and communication, and a scattering of Jewish communities throughout the Mediterranean world. Mary heard that she was a favored one and would be a vehicle of God's gift to the world. She responded, "Here am I, the servant of the Lord; let it be with me according to your word" (Luke 1:38). Then as she watched the unfolding development and ministry of Jesus, she "treasured all these words and pondered them in her heart" (Luke 2:51). Her faithfulness and pondering wisdom led the infant church in Jerusalem to count her among its respected leaders.

Sometimes the timing for a selection is conditioned by chaos and even conflict. For John Mark, the road to leadership was a rocky and conflicted one. The timing was dictated by the opportunity for Paul and Barnabas to revisit new churches in Asia Minor in a second missionary journey. They wanted and needed companions and associates but could not agree about one who had failed them on a previous trip. The conflict occasioned some choices, which were verified years later by experience, maturity, and reconciliation.

A BIBLICAL WITNESS

from John Mark, a Selectee
(based on Acts 12:12; 13:5; 13; 15:36-39; Colossians 4:10;
2 Timothy 4:11; Philemon 24; and 1 Peter 5:13)

My selection as a leader and worker in the enterprise of Christ was certainly not a smooth one, and that is an understatement. The selection was tumultuous and full of anxiety—for both me and those who selected me.

What irony! Our church in Antioch had just received two emissaries from the great Jerusalem Council who bore a letter, bringing news of encouragement. The letter told how their wisdom "seemed good to the Holy Spirit and to us" (Acts 15:28). We were all impressed with the way that the Spirit of God brought a real sense of unity to the mind of the church over a potentially explosive issue.

So immediately after that we were surprised when Paul and my cousin Barnabas, led to revisit the churches on a second missionary journey, fell into a heated argument that centered on me! To put it simply, Barnabas wanted to take me along and

Paul did not. These two giants of missionary initiative were split down the middle over my selection. Both said their prayers. Both loved and cared for the church intensely. Both had a vision for what needed to be accomplished on this visit. Both had experience in personnel matters—nurturing new leaders in the faith. They regarded each other with respect and high esteem, yet they could not agree. Their disagreement became so sharp that they parted company. Paul took Silas. Barnabas took me.

In the swirl of controversy, I'm not sure I am the one to sort it all out. Paul's objection was rooted in my desertion of them in the first journey, when I went back to Jerusalem. I had been serving as a sort of apprentice, assisting them along the way. Sure, I was young. I will never forget the excitement our house experienced that night when Peter showed up at the door, interrupting our all-night prayer meeting. My mother, Mary, was a host and leader in this little house church, so I had had a solid formation time.

Maybe some of the luster had worn off during that first journey. Perhaps I was just immature. I may have yearned to visit the mother church in Jerusalem to connect with James, Mary, and other sisters and brothers.

But when I observed that Jerusalem Council and the way the Spirit moved them to a decision, I wanted to reenlist, so I went to Antioch and volunteered my services—thus inadvertently becoming the eye of a storm!

In recent years I have come to some wisdom and consolation over the matter, and Paul has too. After serving well with Barnabas (who also had been Paul's mentor), Paul invited me to assist him in Rome while he was under house arrest. The Spirit had given him some second thoughts, mellowed his temperament, and opened his heart to my unique gifts. He wrote kind and affirming words about me in his letters to the faithful. I guess nothing is ever lost in the economy of God's love and grace. God used the timing of that argument back in Antioch to further the work—to grow me into a more effective servant, to grow the church, and to deepen the heart of one of God's great leaders.

❖

For This Church

In framing an issue for discernment, our question is not only directed to God, seeking God's will above all else, but also placed in the context of a specific setting and time. We are to select leaders, but for what kind of church? The way organizations operate is changing so much as we enter the twenty-first century that we need to give serious attention to—and even speculate about—the future. We cannot select leaders for a church of the past but must prepare for the church of the future, into which the Spirit is breathing new life and stretching boundaries.

One cannot get a grip on the church of the future without considering the church's past. If a congregation is going to look ahead, it must first consider its own history and come to an understanding of its own story. In our work with the development of church boards, we identified four basic practices—storytelling, biblical/theological reflection, envisioning the future, and spiritual discernment. These practices are detailed in *Transforming Church Boards into Communities of Spiritual Leaders* (see Resources). We found that the four practices are interrelated, interactive, and interdependent. A church does not choose only one practice out of a grab bag. These particular exercises must of necessity work together. So looking to the future always begins with looking to the past. Every congregation has its own story line and from that develops its own song. Look at the founding stories. Look at the stories of new beginnings. Look at the times the church seemed to be stuck. Look at the lay and clergy leaders who seemed to bear the identity of the church symbolically in their own persona. Look at the ways the church has faced (or not faced) adversity, conflict, windfalls, and challenges in the community and world. Every church has a story line, a narrative theme, a defined ethos or character, a set of values and beliefs, and a song that it will carry into its future—if not consciously then unconsciously.

So always begin the discernment process by framing the issue in the context of story. What is your story? The congregation is a spiritual community. The spirit of a congregation may be healthy and life-enhancing, or it may be diseased and fallen, thereby life-depleting. What is the story line of that development and expression?

Let's take a look at congregational life from the perspective of persons who deal with organizational life in parachurch, ecumenical circles. Loren Mead, founder of The Alban Institute, presented a striking contrast between the past and the present in *The Once and Future Church*, a contrast that has ongoing relevance. Looking back, he sees a church of "Christendom," a church operating within a culture that supported and reinforced the organization. That is the "once" church. Today that church-culture relationship does not exist. The "future" church is yet unclear, for the new church is still being forged. In the meantime, we are to engage in basic practices of formation until the new patterns are revealed. Churches often still select leaders as though members were living in the old paradigm, but they need leaders for the transitional time. These new leaders will possess a different and unique set of gifts and skills that do not match the set called for when organizational and operational patterns in the church were more predictable.

A changing view of organizational life is emerging also from the perspective of voices in the social sciences of leadership and management. In the spring of 2000, Leadership Network of Dallas, Texas, convened a gathering in Colorado under the umbrella title "Exploring off the Map." The organizers called in prominent leaders in the field to think together with church folks about the future shape and patterns of the church. The timing and theme were keyed to the two-hundredth anniversary of the Lewis and Clark expedition—a journey that literally explored uncharted territory.

Organizational scientists like Peter Drucker, Peter Senge, Margaret Wheatley, and Charlotte Shelton offer insights that are helpful for assessment of the church's character—both today and tomorrow. These authors posit a very fluid and dynamic understanding of institutions. In *Dance of Change*, Peter Senge describes organizations as organic gardens rather than machines. Margaret Wheatley looks at organizations from the viewpoint of the Newtonian physics of cause and effect, of predictability and stability, and of quantum physics, in which chaos and dynamic energy forge patterns conditioned by "strange attractors." She suggests that we look for the edges of energy in organizations, go there, and ask, "How do we tap into that energy?"[3]

Affirming these dynamic understandings of organizational life, Charlotte Shelton suggests that new capacities of leadership are elicited as well. She calls for leadership that includes "the heart's intelligence . . . wisdom . . . and intuitive ways of knowing, *learning from the inside out.*"[4]

The voices of biblical theologians also bring insight into the future of the church by examining the changing nature of the church in its current context. Old Testament scholar Walter Brueggemann likens the church of the new millennium to the experience of Israel in the Exile. In his lectures in China, published as *Gathering the Church in the Spirit*, he asserts that all the familiar trappings of Israel's faith—the land, city, Temple, and rituals—had been removed in the Exile. God's people found themselves in a strange, hostile, and alien culture. So they began claiming their story, forming it around numerous voices that were sometimes out of harmony with one another. But they were willing to allow those stories to lie side by side while they sought to discern their own identity and call by the spirit of Yahweh.

A seminar participant once asked us to identify a biblical image that would reveal insight into the current time in which the church exists. We responded, "The Exile." "Yes," he persisted, "but what part of the Exile? Are we just entering, having been torn from our familiar roots? Or are we in deep depression about the fleeting good old days? Or are we beginning to recover our story? Or are we see-ing a new vision as a servant people? Or are we scheming strategies for recovery? Or are we back in the city, beginning to rebuild the walls? Or are we dealing with the resistance—both external and internal—to the formation of a new kind of church?" Any church would benefit from dealing with this very good set of questions! We pass them on to you and the leadership of your church for your own discernment.

The changes in the nature and practice of leadership will affect your decisions when you are invited to select new leaders. Take a close look at your faith community—its history, current life, and future shape—to determine "what wants to happen here now." Even though Loren Mead does not offer crystal-clear predictions of what "future church" will look like, profound contrasts with the "once church" are emerging. Here are some that we see:

1. *A difference in the way groups are formed and cultivated.* Congregations will form groups for the short term rather than regarding established groups as permanent entities. Groups will be birthed out of vision, need, and call. They will exist as long as there

are several vision bearers within the group and as long as the group pursues its goal and mission. Groups have a predictable lifetime: forming, defining, struggling, engaging, and declining. Congregations will see themselves as gatherings of groups as well as of individuals. The congregation will birth, cultivate, nurture, release, and close groups. Leadership within this atmosphere of vital groups will be different from that within an organization of static, often obsolete, groups.

2. *A difference in the way a church is organized.* Organizational charts with firm authority and accountability lines characterize the "once" church. Granting permission will characterize the future church. In place of the tightly organized plan generated by leaders from the top and then passed down in the "once" church, the gifts and unique callings of the people in the future church will generate many new initiatives. New leaders will be the gardeners who can identify seeds of call, help people gather in groups around those calls, find ways to create a spiritual community on mission, and reflect biblically and theologically about where God is present in the midst of their ministries. Then the leaders will facilitate celebration and worship growing out of their life and ministry together.

3. *A difference in the way communication takes place.* In this information age, individuals and congregations will go wherever they want to get the help and information to do the work to which God calls them. They can look beyond the resources offered by their own church, denomination, or religious tradition. Denominational control will decrease when helpful stories, designs, models of ministry, and practical tools are readily available from many sources. New leadership will give permission to seek out new sources, help with assessment and evaluation skills, and be willing to broker information from various origins.

4. *A difference in the way decisions are made.* Rational, analytical, and "winning" convictions have dominated "church past." Now we see just how controlling Western ways are. Our parliamentary culture is biased in favor of rational, linear, verbal, and assertive people and against those who come to and express wisdom through hunch, intuition, story, solitude, pictures, and imagination. The pressure to seek more inclusive decision-making ways grows as the decision-making gifts of women, peoples of the developing nations, racial and ethnic minorities, and Generation Xers are recognized. If, as Sister Mary Benet McKinney says, "everyone has some of the wisdom," then we will find ways to sit together in patient, prayerful discernment. Seeking consensus in this way will introduce a whole new culture of decision making in the church.

5. *A difference in the way mission is planned.* The old way of managing by objective, in which goals and objectives are charted, is giving way to a much more fluid approach of looking to the edges of energy. Those edges might be seen through vision, pain, or yearning. Instead of making our plans, asking God to bless them, engaging in them in order to prove that we are worthy in God's sight, we look for signs and signals of God's presence in the world and then go to those places of energy. We are invited into a dance—often unpredictable but surely exciting. Only a very different style of leader can enter this dance!

6. *A difference in the way to consider one's calling.* In "church past" a call was seen to be the property of the ordained or specially gifted church professionals. Only a few had a *real* call. But now let us assume that all are called. The discernment will not focus on whether or not one has a call. The discernment will attempt to distinguish what each person's calling is. Leaders elected for future church will be those who have probed their own calling and who have the

capacity to stand or sit with others who are engaged in discerning their own call. These leaders might be considered midwives who birth vocations in ministry.

7. *A difference in the way we do theology.* In "once church," theology had been worked out in other arenas and organized into systems of thought, category by category. Then those thought systems were communicated via teaching and preaching to folks who were to learn the theology. In "future church," the stories and experience of the groups in the church will be valued and shared in their own right. The tradition expressed in the biblical stories will be laid alongside those stories, and from that juxtaposition meanings, values, and beliefs can surface. The theologies of other generations, eras, geographical locations, and the ecumenical world will be placed in dialogue with these current theologies, tempering and affirming the unity of the church.

Leaders for future church will recognize that they are to engage in theological reflection, not just swallow what has been passed down. And they will facilitate theological reflection by others who are weighing their own experiences in light of the gospel. Theology will not be compartmentalized into categories such as mission, evangelism, stewardship, education, pastoral care, or liturgy. It will be holistic and related to the points where God is present in the midst of the church.

We see that framing the leadership question for spiritual discernment needs to be placed in the context of the kind of future church to which leaders are called. A whole new direction is to be discovered. We are not just filling slots on the organizational chart of a mechanistic organization. We are, rather, seeking to find whom God is calling to provide spiritual leadership for a kind of church whose wineskins are not only soft but are still being formed.

A WITNESS FROM LIFE IN
FUTURE CHURCH

Missouri West Conference of The United Methodist Church

Out of a concern that the Board of Ordained Ministry was approaching its selection process more in the manner of a secular screening process than a spiritual discernment of callings, the board scheduled a two-day retreat for the selectors and candidates with the theme "Discernment and the Wesleyan Means of Grace."

A nearly equal number of candidates and board members gathered to engage together in basic practices of spiritual formation and discernment: prayer, worship, small-group discernment, shared stories of spiritual journeys, common meals, Bible study, spiritual direction/companioning, solitude, teaching from the Wesleyan heritage, and Communion. Rather than the board's meeting to interview and vote to accept or reject each candidate, members of the whole community were invited to explore their respective callings, whether that would lead to ordination or not. Board members affirmed that each Christian has a special calling.

Dr. Paul Jones, a participating board member, observed, "When the written evaluations were read, several things had become clear. The priority had shifted to where it belonged: God does the calling, and ours is the task of faithful discernment of the Spirit's leadings. For this, spiritual preparation for each board member was necessary. Discernment of 'specks' requires a prior wrestling with the 'log' in one's own eye. Finally, we parted, but not as individual teams who had dealt with isolated individuals. Having functioned organically as the body of Christ, no candidate could enter the conference as a stranger. Sixty-two persons had become partners in ministry."

Although this story comes from a judicatory level in the setting of a two-day retreat, the same dynamics and practices could occur at the congregational level. We believe that folks yearn for special times and places to engage in spiritually rooted, prayerful process. That process could take place over a series of meetings at home as well as during a concentrated retreat.

2

READYING FOR SPIRITUAL
DISCERNMENT

Discernment as Church Culture

BEING FORMED IN A CULTURE OF BIBLICAL DISCERNMENT

For a selection team to engage in a process of spiritual discernment, discernment must be a way of life for the congregation as a whole, for the team in particular, and for each individual who is deliberating. This preferred culture does not come naturally or easily. The church has a tendency to ape the culture around it and borrow selection and decision-making ways from the world. Typically we do business the way the world of business, education, or government operates. Very early in life we learn ways of advocating, prevailing, and playing the political power games to gain one's own advantage. We have learned to align our self-interests with candidates who can return the favors we have craftily bestowed or who can enhance our own agenda.

Those ways easily spill over into our church nominating rooms, creep onto our selection tables, and infiltrate our circles of deliberation. These tendencies have been more fully described in the section on "creeping cultures" in *Transforming Church Boards* and the history of accommodation in *Discerning God's Will Together* (see Resources).

45

In this chapter we have chosen the word *formed* carefully and deliberately. Christian *formation*, rooted in Catholic tradition, is a deeper and more profound concept than Christian *education*, which comes out of mainline Protestant tradition with its historic emphasis on education at all levels of the church and culture. To be "in formation" means that one goes beyond the assimilation of knowledge. The process of formation combines practices with accrued knowledge, shaping one's character over a lifetime.

A glimpse into the lives of Miriam and Timothy will reveal how important formation of a spiritual way of life really is! Such spiritual grounding becomes a "DNA" that finds expression in all of life.

A BIBLICAL WITNESS
from Miriam, a Selectee
(based on Exodus 2:1-10; 15:20-21; Numbers 12)

From my birth I was made aware of my identity and destiny as a Hebrew in a foreign land. As a small child I had to think and act quickly when my baby brother, Moses, was floating between life and death on the banks of the Nile River. I helped negotiate the terms of his survival, and this took some initiative and courage on my part. To this day I am proud of what I did.

Water seems to be the prime symbol that formed and expressed my calling in life. In later years I led the Israelites through the water to freedom. You should have seen all Pharaoh's horses, chariots, and drivers in the midst of the sea! God saw to it that we passed through the waters, and I affirmed God's guidance in my own style, leading all the women in song and dance on the banks of the Sea of Reeds.

Of course my life hasn't always been so dramatic, but I

have stirred a few other waters. I did join Aaron in criticizing Moses for his leadership style, and we resolutely claimed equal authority with him. Since when has God spoken only through Moses! This declaration cost me support. I became like a leper. Even Moses came around and tried to reconcile the situation, but I was banished from the camp for seven days.

Though some people probably still think of me as a disobedient and justifiably punished woman, I suspect I'll be remembered as a leader who had the people's support. I know in my heart and head that God chose me to get into trouble, and even to cause some trouble. Hmmm . . . maybe someday I'll even be called a prophetess. It really will be difficult for history to squash singing, dancing, and celebrating the waters of liberation.

A BIBLICAL WITNESS

from Timothy, a Selectee
(based on Acts 16 and 1 Timothy)

I wondered if I had been selected on the rebound. When things don't work out by the book, the next person who comes along may be selected just to fill the slot. Paul and Barnabas had had a falling-out over whether to select John Mark as part of the leadership team for a new missionary journey. John Mark previously had shown his immaturity when he left an earlier expedition. Paul and Barnabas split up. Paul proceeded on his own and soon came to my hometown of Lystra.

Paul spotted me immediately, having learned that I was a disciple. But he was interested in more than my discipleship. My mother was a Jew, and my father was Greek. Paul was looking for an assistant who would be acceptable to both camps, and I fit the bill. He had me circumcised, even though the recent decision of the Jerusalem Council did not require circumcision. His main concern was continuing to witness and strengthening the churches he was about to visit.

When Paul looked for leadership in younger persons, he wanted to know their faith heritage and their spiritual formation. He appreciated the faith of my mother, Eunice, and my grandmother Lois. But he had little patience for those who strutted their endless genealogies or meaningless talk. He looked for a deeper "divine training" that would produce love "that comes from a pure heart, a good conscience, and sincere faith" [1 Tim. 1:4, 5].

Some years later I came to understand Paul's motivation as I read and reread his letters to me about selecting church leaders. He looked for the fruits of this divine training that had been formed by the Spirit of God. He wrote that bishops were to be temperate, sensible, respectable, hospitable, teachers, gentle, and good managers. Deacons were to be serious, not greedy, experienced, and full of faith. Women leaders needed to be serious, temperate, and faithful as well [1 Tim. 3].

Often those who select leaders automatically eliminate young persons as being too immature or inexperienced. But Paul really did not hold my youth against me. "Let no one despise your youth, but set the believers an example in speech and conduct, in love, in faith, in purity" [1 Tim. 4:12].

I have taken those words to heart. While living out those words in various faith communities, I found a wonderful excitement and response from many folks who seemed delighted to affirm my leadership role in their midst.

Craig Dykstra draws attention to the important place of "practices" in formation:

Practices are those cooperative human activities through which we, as individuals and as communities, grow and develop in moral character and substance. They have built up over time and, through experience and testing, have developed patterns of reciprocal expectations among participants. They are ways of doing things together in which and through which human life is given direction, meaning, and significance, and through which our very capacities to do good things well are increased. And because they are shared, patterned, and ongoing, they can be taught. We can teach one another how to participate in them. We can pass them on from one generation to the next.[1]

Peter Senge, in presentations to the "Exploring off the Map" conference, commented that the best-selling books purchased by Generation X young adults fall into the categories of (1) the new economy, and (2) Buddhism. The new economy serves their aspirations to become wealthy—something that works to their own immediate advantage. Buddhism, he points out, is more a religion of practice than of creed and dogma. Buddhism interests the under-thirty crowd because engaging in its practices affects their own formation. Senge comments that only a very small percentage (perhaps 5 percent) of Christians embrace Christianity for its formative practices. People usually adopt Christianity for its system of beliefs and moral values.

Spiritual discernment is one of several practices that were pushed aside in favor of more efficient, power- and control-oriented decision-making processes. Discernment has a rich biblical heritage; it was practiced, reflected upon, and written about by early church forebears. Generally practiced in the relative seclusion of religious communities, discernment occasionally was taken up in the life of various faith traditions. But the practice has not been well understood. A common language has not been developed around discernment, nor are people immediately comfortable with the basic concept. It is ironic that faith communities do not access this rich gift with such a long and deep heritage because it seems "so foreign"! The church's recent fascination with spirituality has opened a window to discernment, allowing Christians to consider again this ancient practice.

Chapter 4 of *Discerning God's Will Together* shows historic connections between discernment and a variety of church traditions, presents discernment as a distinct culture alongside other culturally oriented decision-making processes, and names ten *movements* that can be used in its practice. A language and vocabulary are becoming more familiar among practitioners of discernment, giving them a way to prepare for, engage in, and reflect upon discernment's meaning.

Introducing discernment into the life of a church requires care and intentionality. Only with such deliberate introduction will discernment become formative for individuals and the church as a whole. *Discernment* is not a substitute word for *choosing*, to be used while a church continues its same old selection methods and cultures. Words become faddish, including *discernment*. It is one thing to use and say the word but quite another thing to live deeply and prayerfully into its practice. Here is one church's experience of introducing a new concept and practice of "discernment."

A WITNESS
FROM A CONGREGATION
Westminster Presbyterian Church, Lincoln, Nebraska

Westminster Presbyterian Church in Lincoln, Nebraska, is a large church comprised of community and university leaders in the state capital. Its members tend to be drawn from the business, educational, political, and civic leadership of the community. They in turn bring leadership selection procedures from their associations in the community at large to the church.

When Carl Horton, associate pastor for spiritual life and growth at Westminster, was attempting to focus his doctoral studies program in spiritual formation, he wanted an initiative that would impact the leadership of the church he was serving. He saw the boards of the church operating predominantly according to a corporate-board model rather than a model of intentional spiritual discernment. Having been aware of the Worshipful-Work model and its emphasis on church boards as communities of spiritual leaders, he consulted others in the congregation about a possible shift. Together they saw a potential starting place in the process of nominating and selecting church leaders. They would invite the nominating committee, as well as those who would be under consideration, into an intentional process of spiritual discernment. Working with the nominating committee in church administration was not within Carl's job description. He soon secured permission to claim that arena as a vehicle for spiritual growth in the church.

Carl and the chairperson of the nominating committee, Deb Schorr, led the committee in putting together the nuts-and-bolts specifics to a sweeping vision of a different way to seek nominations. They wanted to move away from the practice of approaching people through cold calls, away from "plugging holes" in church-officer vacancies to a deeper level, a consideration of calling to ministry.

The existing mission statement of the nominating committee reflected the congregation's selection culture. It was tied to fulfilling the requirements of the *Book of Church Order* and the bylaws about recruiting members to fill positions. The new and revised mission statement stated that the committee was to "discern those whom God is calling to positions of leadership in our congregation." Furthermore, the committee would invite the nominees into a process of discernment.

In addition, Carl and Deb redefined the leadership roles of the church in terms of spiritual leadership. Elders were to be known as "spiritual leaders." Deacons would be known as "servant leaders." Both elders and deacons would engage in service and care. Ushers would be known as "hospitality leaders." The foundation trustees would be known as "stewardship leaders." And the nominating committee would be known as "representative leaders." The changes in the mission statement, laced with biblical references and connections, were adopted by the session of the church, thereby institutionalizing the shift in the selection culture.

At least that change in mission statement and nomenclature was a starting place. Along the way Carl and Deb would need to continue to teach and interpret, especially at those junctures of prevailing habits, resistance, or misunderstanding. Upon that foundation, the first nominating committee was invited into an understanding and experience of discernment. Committee members soon discovered that this way would differ from the usual, and some were hesitant to try it. One member resigned. Getting people on board took some interpreting and even selling! The committee's habit had been to bring the church pictorial directory to a meeting in order for members to spot persons they recognized, then complete their selection task as quickly as possible.

At the first meeting of the nominating committee, Deb and Carl presented the new mission statement, introduced the redefined leadership roles, and emphasized the place of gifts for ministry. Instead of plunging into the pictorial directory and getting to task, the committee was led in an extended period of prayerful reflection, contemplating personal stories.

While in prayer, committee members thought about people who had touched them in their own lives. They identified aspects of leadership that might create spiritual models. They considered who might have those qualities in the church right now, letting God reveal faces, activities, and characteristics. They then gave thanks to God for the qualities in those persons who had been so influential. To prepare for the next meeting, each committee member was to engage in prayerful discernment individually at home.

Sensing the importance of everyone's being on the same page as the church embarked on a new path, the committee requested that the congregation hear a sermon coinciding with their learnings and work preached from the pulpit. The committee also used various church newsletters and bulletins to educate the membership on the new process. During that first year naysayers expressed reservations about a spiritual rather than a political process. They feared that the process would be too public, too cumbersome, or too lengthy.

Each member of the nominating committee went home from the first meeting with a packet, a kind of workbook on discernment. The book contained an introduction to discernment, pointers on discerning prayer, a timeline for the work of the committee, a reading list, and a way for each member of the committee to engage in the next step of prayerful discernment. Before the second meeting, everyone was to spend five different thirty-minute segments of time in prayer—one for each of the five leadership groupings. They were to ask some of the same questions that they had experienced in the first prayer gathering, only allowing names to come to them.

When the members of the committee gathered again, they shared the fruits of their personal discernment. They read scripture together. They prayed for those who were discerning God's will. At this gathering they engaged in a group (rather than individual) discernment process. The meeting was blanketed in prayer. They shared the names that had surfaced in their private prayer and talked about qualities that had become important to them. They identified those to whom God was leading them, looking for overlaps and repeating names. They were urged not to limit their selection based on known or assumed personal circumstances of the candidates, such as pregnancy, job change, busy schedule, and so on. They understood that each person should have the chance to decide for herself or himself rather than having that opportunity to decide taken away.

Once the committee had prayerfully generated its list, each name on the list was assigned to the nominating committee member who had felt some connection to that person. Committee members were oriented on how to make contact on behalf of the committee. They would not ask for a decision in the initial contact; rather, prospects would be urged to say maybe and to enter into a discernment process. A number of the prospects said no for familiar reasons, but some noes came because individuals were not comfortable with a spiritual process. Those selectees who did agree to the discernment process received a letter inviting them to consider a specific role for ministry. The letter included a schedule for meeting in small groups in "home gatherings."

Two different members of the nominating committee hosted each of the home gatherings. Ten to twelve potential nominees gathered in each of eight groups—scheduled to allow attendance at a variety of times for one hour. Each person received a copy of the ministry positions and clear information about participating in discernment. The nominating process was explained, and all were invited into a discernment process along the same lines of questioning and reflective prayer that the nominating committee members had experienced.

In the home gatherings the selectees saw other members who had been invited into discernment. This gathering contrasted with the secrecy that shrouded the work of prior committees and their nominees. The prospects were a mixture of persons, each of whom was asked to consider one particular ministry in the five ministry areas.

Together the selectees and nominating committee hosts considered scripture and explored gifts for ministry. The selectees identified people who modeled ministry for them. They thought about questions such as: "To what is God calling you?" "Is this the time to share your gifts with the church?" They were asked to pray about their response and given a discernment process sheet to help them listen attentively to the Spirit. They were to contact the person who had invited them within forty-eight hours if possible, responding yes, no, or I need more time.

When a prospect responded with a no, the committee respected that answer. Then, gathering in prayer, the committee went to another name that had surfaced at an earlier discernment session.

All the while, the chair of the committee, Deb, promoted positive conditions for the effectiveness of the process by being actively involved and open to the participants. She, along with the committee, experienced both the highs and the lows of the process. They were surprised by the number of negative responses—especially after the prayer gatherings. Deb and the committee learned that some people were uncomfortable with the prayer orientation, with meeting in homes, and particularly with the practice of sitting in silence.

The leadership and discernment process has evolved over four years since its introduction. During the first two years Carl, the associate pastor, was an active leader. During the third year he trained others to lead the process while providing the resources for committee leaders. During the fourth, the leaders handled the whole process on their own.

What were the results of this discernment initiative? Participants sensed God's presence in the process. The practice of active prayer related to the committee's mission was perceived as positive. The sense of call was considered at the outset of the process. The committee, the potential candidates, and the congregation as a whole grew in their understanding of discernment. Those selectees who said yes were more devoted to their new work. Those who entered into service through the door of discernment would practice that art later as they met, interacted, decided, and worked in their areas of ministry. The nominating committee benefited by becoming a community of prayer. The members drew closer to one another as they spent meaningful time together.

The story of Westminster Presbyterian Church offers some important learnings. A new culture of selection was established. This change could not have occurred if the effort had occurred on the periphery of the congregation—or even within the educational "program;" instead, the discernment process adopted by the nominating committee affected the whole church system at its heart and core. A concern was named; a vision was lifted up. Through teaching and preaching, the practice of discernment was broadcast to the whole membership of the church. An effective facilitator modeled discernment and gave participants an opportunity to experience it firsthand. The whole congregation developed a language through which members could reflect and communicate. Leaders were trained, and resources were produced and made available for follow-up work by individuals. Those resources would be used in subsequent years. All these components were indispensable to shifting the culture of selection.

Will the new culture last? Will a new pastor affirm it? Will the vision of the original participants continue? Will different leadership allow the church to back off and utilize a less rigorous process? Time will tell.

ROOTING IN BIBLICAL TRADITION

When we say that a congregation needs to be formed in a culture of biblical discernment, we refer to one of the ten movements explained fully in *Discerning God's Will Together* called rooting: "Rooting in the tradition connects religious and biblical stories, themes, and images with the situation at hand. The tradition may confront, confirm, nudge, or even transform the direction of the discernment process."[2] Our own personal and congregational stories are to be placed in dialogue with the longer and deeper story. From the wisdom that flows from such dialogue people can make selections and choices.

After five years of strategic preparation, the Reformed Church in America made a significant decision at its Pentecost General Synod Meeting in June of 2000. Upon recommendation of their general secretary, Wes Granberg-Michaelsen, the church committed to making decisions in the future via "biblical discernment."

Delegates to the meeting voted

to arrange the schedule of General Synod 2001 to enable delegates to engage in biblical discernment through small group Bible study and reflection groups focused on important issues [without adding time or cost] and further to consider ways for permanently changing the structure and means of decision making for General Synod so that biblical discernment and implementation of local and global mission will always receive a priority of time and attention in the agenda . . . and further to encourage consistories, classes, and regional synods to expand their pursuit of discernment-style decision making and space for shared biblical reflection and also to adequately prepare their representatives to each General Synod.[3]

The use of the word *biblical* was intentional. Using the term was more than a political ploy to satisfy the biblical watchdogs of the Synod. The usage recognized that their own grand reformed tradition, "reformed and always reforming," is rooted in the soil of the Holy Scriptures. Note also that the whole church as a system was included as an arena for an intentional practice of spiritual discernment. A change like this could not happen at just one level in the church. This change needed to permeate the whole in order to create a new culture of decision making.

To root in biblical discernment does not mean that the selection process is held hostage to literalistic proof-texting—fastening upon one dearly held text that validates a particular position. No, biblical discernment invites members of a community of faith to grapple with one another's perspective and with the biblical witness in its entirety, trusting that the Spirit will lead them into God's wisdom.

In comparing today's church to Israel in exile, we note that the recovery of Israel's story did not reduce it to one voice; rather, a plurality of stories lay alongside one another. Within those blended or even discordant stories the spirit of Yahweh spoke a prophetic word. In selecting leaders through discernment today, we are to root our process in story, laying biblical story alongside biblical story. When we draw upon those stories we are putting them in dialogue with one another, with our current contextual stories, and with the spirit of God. Opening to the will, yearning, and call of God can lead us to the conclusion that remains in essence a mystery: "seemed good to the Holy Spirit and to us." This hard, patient, and prayerful process is far from simplistic proof-texting. It will open us to our own doubts and fears as well as to our own hopes and faith.

LETTING GO—THE HEART OF SPIRITUAL DISCERNMENT

Engaging in deep, spiritually centered discernment will invite some letting go—both on the part of the selectors as they grapple with one another and on the part of the potential selectee. Shedding, or coming to indifference to anything but God's desires, tugs at the heartstrings, where our emotional investments lie. "Not my will but your will be done" never has been an easy mantra to recite! As we look, for instance, at Elijah the selector and Elisha the selectee, we will see that they both had to do some "letting go."

A BIBLICAL WITNESS

from Elisha, a Selectee,
(based on 1 Kings 19)

I was minding my own business—plowing in my father's fields with a yoke of oxen, when a strange yet familiar man approached. When he stopped, I recognized him. Who wouldn't? He was the famous prophet of Israel, Elijah—one who stood up against King Ahab and Queen Jezebel. He finally had come out of hiding. I was surprised to see him, for the queen had put a price on his head. I ran to greet him but stopped short when, without a word, he took off his prophet's mantle and threw it over me. Overwhelmed, I knew what this action meant. Somehow this man of God saw something—perhaps what neither one of us fully understood—and selected me to be a prophet in his place.

And quite frankly, I'm not so sure that I welcomed the mantle. Word was out that Queen Jezebel was killing anyone who claimed to be a prophet of Yahweh. Yet I also felt attracted to this calling, and I wanted to know more. "Could we talk?" I asked. "Certainly," responded Elijah, "let me tell you how I was drawn to you.

"I was tired, depressed, and ready to give up. Sure, I was on top of my world when God's fire prevailed over the priests of Baal. But that satisfaction was short-lived, as many triumphs are. I ran as far and as fast as I could. In exhaustion I remembered a sacred place, the mountain where our father Moses met God face-to-face. I went to the safety and solitude of that place and quieted down. I faced the wind, felt an earthquake, and saw the power of fire. But then out of the following stillness that fell upon me over an extended period of days, thoughts began to surface. Impressions repeatedly rolled over me. Not many words formed on my tongue. I saw that I was not alone. Thousands had not bowed the knee to Baal. But God wanted leaders—in a foreign land, in the nation of Israel, and for the faithful religious. You came to my mind over and over again.

"Why? I'm not sure. I knew about your father's house, your faithfulness and steadfastness and your reputation among your neighbors. So here I am. And here you are. And here God is. In the name of this Holy God I ordain you as prophet. If the same spirit of the living God rests on you, show it in some definitive act."

What was I to do? Eleven other farmers who were driving yokes of oxen were watching, as were the neighbors. I sensed that my response could not be private. It had to be public. It had to be more than show. It had to invite the community's embrace, support, and blessing. The final test would be the sanction of the community. After all, these people knew me and sensed what God was about.

So I gave up my oxen. I created a feast. By slaughtering my two oxen I turned my back on a former vocation and life and made a clean break with the past. The wood from the yokes made a good fire on which to roast the meat. I invited my neighbors to come and eat with me. If they thought I had lost all my marbles and was way out in left field, they would show disapproval by refusing to eat with me. But if they came and ate, they would be blessing the calling from God that Elijah's coat had signified.

The neighbors came. They ate. They listened to Elijah's story. They heard me articulate formerly hidden and latent wonderings. They praised God. And they encouraged me— even offered to plow my tract of land to support my ministry. I honestly can't tell you what had the deeper impact—Elijah's gesture or my friends' affirmation and confirmation. One was a mystical sign, the other a very human act. Now that I have had time to reflect on it, both were important. They worked hand in glove to move me into a new place of leadership.

The invitation to relinquish and let go becomes a call to conversion. Few selectors, when they say yes to serving in a leadership capacity, are aware that they will be called upon to give up and let go of preconceived notions, pet candidates, or their self-created picture of the perfect candidate. "What seems good to me" and "what seems good to the Spirit" may clash. Selectors may be so tempted to forge ahead with their own plans that the Spirit hardly gets a word in edgewise. But the word will get in somehow, and when it does, surrender and letting go will be required.

The movement of *shedding* is one of the first described in *Discerning God's Will Together*. "Shedding means naming and laying aside anything that will deter the person or group from focusing on God's will as the ultimate value."[4] That description serves as an early warning signal, establishes a language, and forecasts what is to come. Selectors may engage in shedding in a perfunctory or tentative way early in the discerning process. That is okay. A group need not go beyond each participant's perceived trust in the community at the outset.

Dietrich Bonhoeffer observed that people come to community with a "wish dream," that is—a picture of what this community is going to do or look like. Then he explains that Jesus will disillusion the group members about their dreams and create a community shaped and held together only by grace.[5] A newly formed selection group might ask one another, "What pictures of the future leadership of this church would you be willing to release in order to allow the Spirit of God to speak?" Other useful questions are "What fears about our selection process or the eventual outcome am I willing to let go of and wrap in the mercy of God?" "When we pray, 'Thy will be done,' what do we need to lay aside to make that a real, heartfelt, prayer?" An open and honest naming of such fears and assumptions can free the Spirit to break in at this beginning point. A ritual may be devised to help the selectors visualize their attachments and the process of letting go. Working with clay or other nonverbal forms of self-examination and expression may work well at this stage. The more difficult relinquishment issues will resurface as the heat gets turned up later in the process; that reality is a natural part of the group's progression as a community.

Some participants may come to the selection table with a clear picture of what the new leader(s) will look like—giftedness, gender, age, experience. Some may come prepared to advocate specific candidates. Some may come planning to repay a favor with a certain selection. People easily become invested and attached to preconceived notions, a circumstance that only heightens the need to shed. Behind and underneath attachments lie subtle ego needs: to win, to prevail, to seek the extension of one's own will. The unconscious ways that people manipulate and posture are slippery ground. The potential for self-deception threatens. When we say, "Seems good to the Spirit and to us," remember that the "us" may have a shadow side that operates in destructive and life-depleting ways. Original sin, the subtle and powerful sin that affects everyone in all aspects of life, might just as easily rise up at the selection table as in some "den of iniquity." If a group is to engage in worshipful work, then the Spirit will lead group members into admission, repentance, confession, forgiveness, release, absolution, and healing.

Failing to come to terms with the latent destructive forces in both individuals and the group as a whole can invite unwanted dynamics and consequences. Those consequences are (1) *isolation*— failing to connect with one another at a heart level and to listen to one another deeply; (2) *division*—aligning into several camps that each consume energy to control or disrupt opposing groups; (3) *projection*— attributing characteristics to other selectors or potential selectees based on personal inadequacies or perspectives; (4) *denial*—refusing to face up to realities in oneself or the current situation; (5) *rigidity*—filtering out good information needed to make a selection.

The following imaginary story by Margaret Benefiel, who teaches and writes from a Quaker tradition, reveals the importance of being formed through relinquishment into servants ready for the task of selection. A long struggle by a search committee may be necessary; eventually, though, the struggle itself graces the selection process when group members genuinely let go of obstacles to the Spirit.

WITNESS FROM A CONGREGATION
from the fictitious Smithtown Pastor Search Committee

What is going on here? If everyone on the search committee earnestly sought God, why did God not reveal which candidate to choose? Were some members not listening to God? Were some stubborn? Perhaps, but perhaps something entirely different was occurring.

In the prayer life of an individual, prayer develops in different ways at different times. Early in the Christian life, a person often experiences abundant blessings, with God's answering every prayer. Later, prayer is not so easy. The Christian finds himself or herself bumping into closed doors or feeling that prayers don't make it past the ceiling. Has she lost her touch? Is he doing something wrong? Not necessarily. Maturing in Christ includes learning the subtleties of prayer and of relationship with God. As spiritual babes, we cry out to God and God answers, letting us know that our cries are heard and that we can count on God. As we grow out of spiritual infancy we discover that God invites us to learn new lessons. We learn to wait. We learn that sometimes we pray for one thing and God, translating our prayers into what we most need, gives us another. We learn to listen to God. We learn to let God shape our prayers. We experience the dark night of the soul, when God seems to have abandoned us. We learn to desire God for Godself and not the gifts God gives.

Just as the individual discovers many twists and turns in the journey toward God, so the committee or Friends meeting or other corporate body discovers similar twists and turns. We live in an individualistic culture, and we Friends have absorbed much of that individualism. Thus, we experiment with "corporateness" tentatively and suspiciously, if at all. Many of our Friends meetings and committees are still spiritual babes when it comes to corporate prayer and discernment, even though these same bodies may contain spiritually mature individuals. When we gather corporately to make a decision and turn to God in prayer, we expect God to answer our prayers in the way we frame them and according to our timetable. Many times we get the answers we expect, as God is so delighted that we want to listen and are praying in our committees at all and is so wanting us to know we have been heard and responded to that God is happy to give us our answers in a form we can recognize. Sometimes, however, we do not receive the answers we expect. Rather than assume that our experiment with corporate discernment has failed or that God has betrayed us or that some people have not been listening to God, might we have eyes to see another explanation? Perhaps God is inviting us to deepen in prayer corporately. Perhaps God is inviting us out of corporate spiritual infancy into corporate maturity.

The committee expected God to answer the question in the way members had framed it: Which of the two candidates was God's choice for the position? While God sometimes answers in the way we expect, sometimes God has something else entirely for us. Perhaps God knew that a third person would be better for the job. Or that Smithtown Friends Meeting needed an interim pastor for a year before it called a long-term pastor. Or that either of the two candidates the search committee has in mind will be fine but that the committee has work to do in learning to respect and trust one another and to listen to God together before any choice will be a good one—or any of a number of other possibilities. Just as in our individual prayer lives when we do not receive the answers we expect or want, we must seek the deeper invitation from God, so it is in our corporate prayer and discernment. Just as in our individual prayer lives we ask God to meet us where we are when we feel frustrated and betrayed by God, so it is in corporate prayer and discernment.

How might the Smithtown pastor search committee have trusted that God knew its needs and understood its timetable? How might the committee members have trusted God to reshape their agenda? Could they have believed that God knew their needs better than they did, and that God's timing in meeting those needs was better than their timing? Might they have considered the points of conflict between the two groups on the search committee, considered the different values those perspectives represented, and brought those different values to God in prayer? What would it have taken for the members of the search committee to name their fears about identifying conflicting values in their midst, their fears about trusting God and trusting one another, their fears about letting go of control of the timetable and the process?

When a group lets go of its agenda and seeks God's agenda, any number of things might happen. In the case of Smithtown, consider the following scenario. After the second meeting of not coming to unity, the group decides to take a hard look at itself, naming the conflicting values represented by the two factions. One segment favors the older, more experienced pastoral candidate, who would bring solid preaching, support a traditional worship service, and work well with the older, longtime members of the meeting. The other segment favors the younger, well-qualified though less experienced candidate, who would bring innovative worship, encourage the ministry of all members, and reach out to newcomers and younger members. The group recognizes that these conflicting values represent a split in the meeting as a whole and that these differences are at the root of many a division in the meeting. Furthermore, the group recognizes that people have always looked to pastoral leadership to resolve conflicts, seeking a pastor who would be all things to all people. No pastor in the meeting's history has filled the bill. People have often blamed their pastors for not providing answers to their problems.

The group decides to seek God in prayer, humbly naming their conflicting values and asking for God's guidance. Someone speaks out of the silence, suggesting that everyone consider the good in the opposing point of view. People speak one by one, naming the good each sees in the values each has opposed, confessing hard-heartedness in closing out others. After two more meetings of continuing to seek God together in prayer, a new solution emerges. The committee calls an interim pastor who specializes in helping meetings with conflicts, and the meeting sets aside the next year as a time to address the different values in its midst, seeking God's guidance for the faith community. Members recognize that they need to do foundational work and name and own their values and direction. They cannot expect a new pastor to do that work for them. They will ask the interim to help facilitate that process.

By seeking God's deeper invitation through the impasse, the Smithtown pastor search committee reached a solution no one would have imagined, a solution that serves the meeting far better in the long run than either of the two options the committee initially framed. Even more importantly, the committee has learned some things together about corporate prayer and discernment: (1) that God can be trusted to work in corporate discernment; (2) that God cares deeply about the meeting as a corporate body and can be counted on to walk with the members through their work together; (3) that the committee members can trust one another to listen to God together and move through tough issues to a place of deeper love and respect and listening, as well as to a solution. Members now possess a stronger foundation for their future work together as a meeting. They have moved out of corporate spiritual infancy and begun the journey toward maturity.

Guiding Principles
in Spiritual Discernment

The early church in Jerusalem was faced with challenges to select leaders. In the following two stories of witness, clear selection matters are framed for prayerful discernment. In each case, the church establishes a set of clear guiding principles from which criteria for their selection are drawn.

from Matthias, a Selectee
(based on Acts 1:15-26)

I am the lucky winner! The draw of the lot determined my selection as one of the twelve apostles. This may seem like a shortcut and an easy way out for a group selecting a religious leader. That was my initial reaction. But having lived into the decision over the passing years, I have great consolation that God was in the whole process.

"How so?" you may ask. The apostles' decision was rooted in tradition. They could very well have proceeded to witness to the life, death, and resurrection of Jesus with eleven or thirteen or whatever number of apostles, but twelve was a sort of magic number—no, a mystical and religious number. The twelve tribes of Israel were lodged deep in Israel's psyche and identity. After all, the growing church would become the "New Israel." In searching the psalms, Peter located a section that read, "Let another take his position of overseer."

The eleven apostles had little experience in selecting leaders. Jesus had done that. But now they were on their own. They confessed to me that they were at a bit of a loss about how to proceed. So they prayed and relinquished their own hold on the process; they gave the matter to God and did what they knew—cast the lot.

The disciples' decision was rooted in experience. They set up a guiding principle. Whoever was selected needed to have been with Jesus from the beginning and a witness to his

Resurrection. That dropped the number down to a more manageable few of us. The apostles searched their own hearts and ours. My name and that of Barsabbas quickly surfaced in their minds. It wasn't so much a "head" thing as it was a "heart" thing.

The apostles' decision was rooted in faith. I wondered where faith was in the drawing of the lot. But they explained to me that both Barsabbas and I were equally qualified and that they could not tip the balance through their own personal assessment. They believed that God had gifted each of us. They believed that no matter who "won the lottery," God would work through this person. So they cast the lot in faith. Barsabbas and I had agreed with them to proceed in this manner. We agreed that the loser would be supportive of the winner. With this unanimity of spirit, the apostles went forward in the confidence that God's will could actually be accomplished! There would be no second-guessing.

Now that I look back on the situation, I realize that my situation was the last recorded use of the lot by the infant church. Pentecost followed closely on the heels of my selection. Jesus had told us that the Spirit would be given, and the Spirit would lead us into all truth. From that point we relied on that presence to interact with our own God-given faculties.

When looking for a replacement for Judas, someone who would round out the apostles' number to twelve, the community determined that whoever would be selected would have "been with us from the beginning and a witness to the Resurrection." That determination certainly limited the field and allowed the disciples to look close at hand for a colleague. That decision on criteria became a guiding principle.

Our experience at Worshipful-Work Center for Transforming Religious Leadership echoes this story. In the initial phase of looking for new leadership for the organization, the Discerning Overseers had to set important selection criteria. Should they conduct a national search and try to match experience and skills with our needs? Or should they limit the search to persons who were part of the Worshipful-Work story and who had experienced personal and/or institutional transformation in that journey? They chose to start with the latter option. It mirrored the Acts 1 story—"One of the men who have accompanied us during all the time that the Lord Jesus went in and out among us, . . . one of these must become a witness with us to his resurrection" (Acts 1:21-22).

The account in Acts 6 of selecting additional leaders to tend the needs of the gentile Christians also chimes a set of guiding principles. These principles revolve around the character of leadership sought. The selectees are to be in good standing, full of the Spirit, and wise. Those selected were persons of deep faith and conviction, as we see in both Stephen the martyr and Philip the evangelist. As we will later see, these same qualities would be found in Philip's daughters who, as prophets who spoke God's word, were commended to the church as well.

When Paul is concerned about shaping the leadership in the apostolic church he counsels Timothy on the criteria to use in selecting bishops. Paul suggests that such an overseer be characterized, among other traits, as temperate, wise, respected, hospitable, adept at teaching and managing, mature, and humble. Qualifications for a deacon are also provided They include being serious, honest, temperate, believing, and hopeful (1 Tim. 3).

When naming the guiding principles that will steer any selecting group, it may be important to consider how the selectees will function as a team together. Many faith communities are moving toward collaborative styles of management and leadership. So finding a good team player or putting together the right combination for an effectively functioning group stretches the selectors to consider a deeper layer of capabilities. They are not just looking for a lone-ranger type of operator. How can the selectors visualize and name mutuality, relationship, and collegiality as guiding principles for the search?

A model based on the Trinity provides a window into an organization with an internal operation that incorporates spirituality. Let's explore how such a vision could help determine criteria—guiding principles—for a selection committee.

Benjamin D. Williams and Michael T. McKibben, who consult with organizations out of a Greek Orthodox Trinitarian orientation, suggest that three key elements for the development of an organization are vision, implementation, and enthusiasm. In their book, *Oriented Leadership,* they connect each of these elements with an image from the Trinity. *Vision* is an image of the Creator God; *implementation* is an image of the Son; and *enthusiasm* is an image of the Holy Spirit.

Many religious traditions work out of a Trinitarian construct, such as the Christian construct of Creator, Redeemer, and Spirit or the Jewish construct of the Torah, land, and community. We respect other traditions but write out of our own Christian tradition, claiming a spiritual heritage that embraces unity within a distinction of roles. We hold a vision of spirituality in leadership that reflects this mystery, looking to the very nature and heart of God. As we posit a collegial and team ministry that reflects a Trinitarian construct, three roles and functions would be important and necessary elements of an understanding and practice of leadership. The guiding principles for leadership will take on Trinitarian roots and expression.

In a pattern drawn from the Trinity, each leader on the team will have distinct identity and roles. Together these leaders model a unifying, loving, and interactive relationship. The Creator loves and expresses a will. The Son's food is to do the will of the Creator. The Spirit opens the eyes and heart of the community to see what God is up to and recognize Christ, who stands in the midst. The Spirit does not call attention to self but is always pointing and saying, "Look over there. See what God in Christ is doing."

Two biblical texts provide foundational insight to this model: Ephesians 1 and Colossians 1. In those texts, the Creator, first person of the Trinity, blesses, chooses, reveals a design, plans, gathers, unifies, and works within the fullness of time. So one function of leadership is to call forth and employ the gifts of those who can bless and affirm the community's story, make strategic choices, plan, care, and tend the life of the organization within an ordered framework of time.

The second person of the Trinity—Servant Redeemer—serves, forgives, grants inheritances, reflects God's image, engages the creation, holds all things together, reconciles earth and heaven (worship and work), and is a locus of God's dwelling. A second function of team leadership is to provide services and resources that put flesh on the particular charism of the organization. Servant leaders who bear the mark and mind of Christ exercise this integrative and reconciling role.

The third person of the Trinity—the Spirit—reveals love, fills with wisdom, stimulates growth and fruit bearing, provides energy and inspiration, and seals the community in word and truth. So a third function of team leadership is to read the signs of the times, listen closely to discern the Spirit's stirring in both social and ecclesiastical cultures, and look for new gifts and callings that may be offered. This "scouting" takes place in a spirit of playfulness, joy, adventure, and excitement. The skills of seeing, naming, and lifting into view the hidden, obvious, or even mysterious edges of a community all draw upon the practices and resources of prayer, discernment, imagination, and enthusiasm. These resources in turn lead to celebration and praise to God's glory!

Here is a rather earthy but appropriate metaphor for the Trinitarian model of a team. In order to progress on the journey, an organization—like a wagon train—needs a trail boss (a trip coordinator), a cook, and a scout. One leads with oversight; one serves with care; and one scouts the edges, alert to opportunity and danger! These roles must interact in a collaborative way. The qualities named for these various roles illustrate important guiding principles in the form of selection criteria.

The following witness, although not written in the context of an intentionally Trinitarian organization, is filled with dynamics that point to the three roles of the Godhead. Read it with Trinitarian eyes! The Reverend Edgar Whelan, rector of an Episcopal parish and chaplain of the diocesan committee to nominate a bishop, describes the committee's discernment process over a nine-month period. He was convinced that the Spirit of God was with the committee as it worked.

A WITNESS
FROM DIOCESAN LIFE
The Diocese of Kansas City

The committee began its long and demanding ministry by agreeing on two beliefs: that Jesus, the Chief Shepherd, knows whom he wants to be our next bishop and that the person he is calling must be a servant. Jesus came and still is among us as one who serves. The committee then saw its task as discovering God's will, which could only be accomplished through a process of discernment.

When a person's mind and spirit are thus freed through prayer, how does God communicate? How does one come to know that mind? In two ways: through the soft voice spoken within, and through careful listening to others.

When in session, our committee stopped frequently each day for both private and common prayer to praise God for being present as we went about God's work, to ask for the Spirit's continued guidance so that what we were considering would truly be God's will, and to thank God for making God's mind known through our work. I also believe that the prayers of the diocese deepened the committee' members' conviction that together we were being freed to do God's will.

To hear the soft voice within, we members of the committee went off by ourselves to read over the material collected and to reflect upon it through prayer. To hear the voice of others, we gathered again in community to share insights through dialogue. Our dialogue involved careful listening to one another. Careful listening entailed setting aside prejudgments, advocacy, and dislikes. Careful listening also meant setting aside the human tendency to debate, because the single goal of debating is to convince others that one's view is the only truth to be considered. Through this careful listening to one another, the members accepted the insights of others as an instrument that God used to manifest God's mind on the matter being considered.

Discernment is the process of seeking out and then following God's will. In order for the process to take place, certain conditions must be met. There must be a deep commitment to discover God's will and then to accomplish it. There must also be a strong belief that God does make God's will known through prayer and careful listening to others.

Many Christians forget that God said, "Your ways are not my ways." They believe that their interests and desires, when held with deep conviction, are precisely what God wants. For too many, discernment means praying for guidance and then entering into hot debates about issues they hold to be important. But discernment begins with the conviction that God's will is not yet known; that the task is to discover it and, once known, to do it. Discernment begins with the conviction that Jesus, the Chief Shepherd, knows whom he wants to be our next servant bishop. It means setting aside self-interests and committing oneself to seeking out Jesus' choice for bishop.

Anyone who has reflected on how our minds work when self-interests, desires, and fears are present, knows how difficult it is to arrive at correct judgments. Here then is the main purpose for prayer in the discernment process. The grace of God is needed if we are to remain indifferent to all but God's will. And it is a grace that God will give through prayer: "Believe me when I tell you, ask and it shall be given to you, seek and you shall find" (paraphrase Luke 11:9; Matt. 7:7).

The discernment process that our committee used was both powerful and holy, especially in the moments of decision—powerful because every decision was made without doubt, dissent, or argument; holy because once a decision was made, it was strongly felt by every member to be the mind and will of God.

3

GATHERING FOR
SPIRITUAL DISCERNMENT

Even rudimentary reflection on the original Pentecost event high-lights a significant truth: The Spirit of God settles upon each indi-vidual disciple in a unique way, but the passion of God's Spirit is released within a communal context. All our stumblings and suc-cesses in forming a variety of communities during our lifetime are nothing short of responses to the Spirit's powerful life and energy with-in, a power beyond human measure. In this chapter, you will be led to reflect deeply upon your unique communal context as you engage in the movements of *listening, exploring,* and *improving.* These move-ments challenge us to see clearly with spiritual eyes and to listen clearly to words, to the silence between words, to nonverbal com-munications. It may be important for selectors to revisit some pre-viously established norms or ground rules before embarking on these movements—ways to pay special attention to the "Spirit" and the "us."

Understanding a Congregation's Story

How has the Spirit of God been moving within the history and char-acter of your faith community? What is the particular ethos of your faith community? In what social and managerial context does your community now exist? What are its operating cultures, and where are the edges of energy? Where will you begin to look for potential candidates for leadership positions?

To reflect on the ethos of your congregation, begin with the story. Put a spiritual magnifying glass to the ethos of the community for whom you are discerning leaders. Since it is easy, given our modern culture, to view a faith community as a hermetically sealed organization that operates like a machine (a machine that breaks down but doesn't change much), it is also easy for us to count heads, material resources, and the number and kinds of groups that a church influences as indicators of its nature. But selectors must ask, "Do these statistics describe the real 'us'? Do these facts reflect whatever it is in us that claims an identity with God's Spirit?" During spiritual discernment, you need the motivation to take a longer and yet closer view of the community the leadership will serve.

Even a microscopic virus can have a significant impact on the health of one or more persons. Keeping that fact in mind as a metaphor, selectors need to take a care-full, prayer-full, real, and engaging yet loving look at the living congregation. The view through the magnifying glass should include the congregation's interaction with its environment and the extent to which it relies on the disciplines of theology and spirituality, as well as its current needs and future visions.

In the ministry of our organization, Worshipful-Work, we often work with leadership groups who seek to "get on the same page," that is, understand how they all have arrived at this moment. They want to comprehend their story inside-out and up-until-now. We suggest they tell the story of their congregation (including the leadership pieces) as each person remembers it or knows of it by using the connecting phrases "and then," and "but before that."[1] We invite a simple telling of the story, leaving reflection for later. We encourage telling the real story with its exciting, humorous, even difficult periods, because all are part of the story. People can come to appreciate even difficult times as graced moments, since deeper awareness usually comes with hindsight—when we see events more clearly.

This storytelling is done in the spirit of Mary Benet McKinney's concept of shared wisdom, developed in *Sharing Wisdom: A Process for Group Decision Making.* Everyone has a piece of the wisdom; no one person has it all. The group reflection on the story is reminiscent of the Stepping Stone Period in Ira Progoff's Intensive Journal Workshop, a process of recording recollections from one's lifetime (such as persons, events, vocation) and turning points or crossroads that took place during those times. Sometimes those personal recollections are brief; at other times lengthy explanations are necessary in order to capture all that is relevant to the event. The beauty of our suggested method of communal storytelling is that others will remember facts and circumstances some have forgotten or have never known.

Some starter questions to prime the pump of communal storytelling might be these: (1) Was the leadership structure always what it is today? (2) How were congregational leaders selected in the past? (3) What do you identify as some of the major challenges past leaders faced? (4) What do you identify as some significant decisions made by your congregational leaders? (5) Who were the people and the events affected by those decisions?

After the story has been told it is important to expand upon it, to listen deeply to it, to name God's presence as revealed in the story, and to further articulate the values and the spirit that inform the selection process. Margaret Wheatley aptly writes about organizational structures (let's substitute for our purpose a particular faith community or congregation): "Each structure has a unique identity, a clear boundary, yet it is merged with its environment. . . . What we observe . . . in all living entities, are boundaries that both preserve us from and connect us to the infinite complexity of the outside world. . . . Not the fragile, fragmented world we attempt to hold together, but a universe rich in processes that support growth and coherence, individuality and community."[2] In reflecting on a congregational story selectors need not limit themselves to exact boundaries but make connections between the story's "inside"—the facts about the congregation—and the story's "soul"—the spirit of the congregation.

Answering questions such as these may be helpful for reflection: (1) In what particularly graced moments did the action and presence of God's Spirit rest on the community? (2) Which decisions were productive and which were counterproductive? (3) What were some points of resistance in decision making? What were some expressions of acceptance? (4) What invisible or "hard-to-grab" influences came into play in those decisions? (5) In what spirit did the community make those decisions—within the arena of known security and control or within the context of a broader spiritual vision? (6) Did we leave anything out of the story? (7) What particular leadership strengths or gifts appear in the story? (8) What truths are evident now, in hindsight? (9) Where do current edges of energy and inner yearnings exist? (10) What situations in the story reinforce the congregation's identity or charism, the invisible structuring that manifests itself in what is held in common within the congregation? (11) Is the congregation programmed toward life (it will do anything, even change, to stay alive) or programmed to wait for the lights to go out? (12) What have we come to appreciate in a new way?

Walter Wink, in his chapter "The Spirits of Institutions" in *The Hidden Spirit: Discovering the Spirituality of Institutions*, writes that every entity has an "angel," the corporate personality or the spirit or essence of the church or institution. He writes that there is an outer form, for example, a congregation's worship space, its programs and meetings, but there is also a deeper level at which the particular spirit or ethos of the community or institution operates. Wink goes on to say that "the angel of an institution is just not the sum total of all that an institution is (which sociology is competent to describe); it is also the bearer of that institution's divine vocation (which sociology is not able to discern)."[3] Engagement in the listening movement of spiritual discernment affords the opportunity to describe the "angel" of the congregation.

Poet Jessica Powers speaks about the "Spirit" and the "us": "God seeks a heart with bold and boundless hungers / that sees itself and earth as paltry stuff; / God loves a soul that cast down all He gave it / and stands and cries that it was not enough."[4] Her words challenge selectors to be hungry for all that God will reveal in discernment, to be attentive to each revelation whether great or small, and to be resilient about new wisdom yet to come. Selectors need not worry about being "tossed to and fro and blown about by every wind" (Eph. 4:14) of influence but rather need to focus on understanding the bigger picture of the congregation and to become empowered by its charism.

Exploration of biblical stories that have some of the same themes, characters, or situations as the congregation's story serves to enlarge the story and often confirms the fact that there's usually more than meets the eye in a congregational story. It's possible that selectors may even experience some spiritual freedom to change course, as happened in Rebekah's story.

from Rebekah, a Selectee
(based on Genesis 24)

An amazing encounter took place one day a number of years ago, a day that started out like most every other day. As was my custom toward evening, I walked down to the nearby spring carrying a large empty jug on my shoulder. While minding my own business, a young fellow came up to me and asked if he could have a sip of water. "Of course," I said, noticing that his clothes were a bit rumpled and rather dusty. I imagined that he had been traveling quite a distance and needed a bit of a respite. So I poured fresh, cold water into his cupped hands and then took great delight in watching his big, refreshed smile. "Let me get water for your camels too," I offered. I made a few trips back and forth from the spring to the trough.

You know how a "sixth sense" takes over when you feel you are being watched? Well, I had this feeling all the while I was watering his camels, but it wasn't a frightening feeling. My sense was that there could be more to this situation than met the eye.

When all the camels were watered this fellow came over to me—even before we exchanged names—and gave me a gold ring on my nose and two shiny gold bracelets for my arm. They were very beautiful, and I was quite taken by his charm and kindness. Then he asked me about my father and whether there was an extra room in my house where he could spend the night. I told him about my family and invited him to be our guest. When he heard my invitation, he bowed and prayed in thanksgiving for God's kindness and for God's leading him to my family. When I heard his prayer, I too was struck by the fact that his initial encounter at the spring was with me rather than with any other person standing in the area. In fact, I was so amazed at our encounter that I almost forgot to refill the water jug before returning home!

When I arrived home I told my brother Laban about the man outside, and Laban rushed back to the spring to escort him and his camels to our house. One servant gave the camels straw to rest on, while another servant brought water so that the guest and our family could wash before sharing a meal.

Amazingly enough, the story of our encounter, and the bigger story of this fellow's entire journey, took precedence over our meal. While the table was being readied the visitor recounted every detail of his journey, beginning with all the earthly blessings God had provided his master, Abraham (my father's uncle), including Abraham's marriage to Sarah and the unexpected birth of their son, Isaac. Next he described the oath he had sworn to Abraham to secure a spouse for Isaac from among Abraham's own kin. The man was a devoted and loyal servant to Abraham, eager to carry out this task, but he realized the job would not be easy to accomplish.

All the while the servant was riding from Canaan to Nahor he was thinking about how and where he might meet some of Abraham's kin. He kept envisioning various scenarios in his head, which only increased his awareness of the enormity of his mission. But then he got in touch with a deeper concern. He realized that he wanted God's assurance of a successful mission. That concern became a prayer as he arrived at the well just outside of town. After securing his camels, he prayed to God, "O Lord, God of my master Abraham, . . . let the girl to whom I shall say, 'Please offer your jar that I may drink,' and who shall say, 'Drink, and I will water your camels'—let her be the one whom you have appointed for your servant Isaac" [vv. 12-14]. He believed that this conversation would be a sign of God's steadfast love for Abraham and a foreshadowing of divine intervention and blessing on the woman's marriage to Isaac.

Our guest also shared some of the advice he'd received from Abraham: "The Lord, in whose presence I have always walked, will send a messenger with you and make your errand successful." He had received sensible caution as well: "If you visit my family and they refuse you, then you are released from this oath." That must have been so comforting!

Well, by now, reality was sinking in. This story was about me! I was the kinswoman Abraham's servant encountered. My family said (almost in unison): "This chance encounter is from the Lord . . . this is far better a situation than we could ever have imagined . . . we cannot get in the way . . . let Rebekah go to Isaac."

More than all the silver, gold, and clothing I received from my family, I appreciated their asking me what I wanted to do in this situation. It was good, noble, and certainly unusual in our culture that Abraham's choice of a spouse for Isaac would be honored only if I sensed God's presence in my selection. Well, I did feel God's leading and presence in this matter, and so I told my mother, brother, and our servants that I wanted to travel to Isaac. I told them that this must be in God's providence. I was at the right place at the right time. All seemed to be under God's guiding hand.

My mother and brother suggested that I stay with them for a few more days before making the long journey to meet my future husband. Following my own heart, I left home the next day. I have been amazed by my life. What at first appeared to be a chance encounter has made all the difference.

It is important for selectors to explore scripture together. As spiritual discerners, selectors hold open space for God's Spirit to move, leaving behind the more familiar analytical ways of making decisions. The habit and practice of spiritual discernment include taking time to grapple with the tension and mystery of being in the presence of God's yearning. Weaving the congregation's story with a scripture story will help to bring clarity, as well as significant questions, to the fore.

Sandra Lommasson, director of the Bread of Life Center for Spiritual Formation in Davis, California, offers a simple, effective way to process a congregation's story through the lens of a scripture story. The following example, described in a letter from Sandra, illustrates the power of guiding statements and questions beginning with "I wonder" or "I notice" used with the scripture reading: "While recently reading the story of Cain and Abel with a pastors' group, we began with 'I notice that Cain and Abel now share the responsibility given to Adam to "tend and to till." . . . I wonder if each chose his work?' And then later, 'I notice that the action of the story begins with an act of worship. . . . I wonder what moved the offering?' And a while later, 'I notice a difference in God's response to the two offerings. . . . I wonder what makes an offering acceptable or unacceptable?'" You can gear "I wonder" and "I notice" statements to specific incidents in a congregation's story or use them to probe deeper into value statements articulated in the story.

There are various ways to weave a congregation's story with a Scripture story. A *lectio divina* form of reading and reflection is a patient, prayerful attention to a passage read aloud, pausing when anyone says, "Please stop." The interval can be full of silence, brief questions directed to God, or reflections on the connections being made between the two stories. What insights into the "Spirit" and the "us" are surfacing? What hymn or refrain seems to fit the moment?

Identifying Desired Qualities for Leaders

At this point in the discernment process, selectors have told the congregation's story and reflected upon it, weaving it with a scripture story. They have pondered the selection of past leaders as well as some of the congregation's major challenges, decisions, and operating cultures. Once selectors have established one or more guiding principles to ground the selection process, the next questions to ask are these: "What qualities, gifts, and skills are we looking for in leaders?" "Where and in whom might we find these particular gifts?"

Sometimes selectors simply neglect to look at persons who are obvious choices right in front of them; other times, they may take great pains to avoid the obvious. Perhaps the daughters of Philip have some wisdom to offer us.

A BIBLICAL WITNESS

from the Daughters of Philip, Selectees
(based on Acts 6; 21:8-14)

We are four in number, but we will speak with one voice because we are unmarried and fully devoted to working with our father in this house church in Caesarea where we have a ministry of speaking for God.

"How does this happen?" folks throughout history have asked (or failed to ask!). "You are women! You have no place in the leadership of the church!" some say. So let us tell our story.

We are named, blessed, and affirmed by the church as prophets. That does not mean we are crazy. Neither have we been shoved into a corner—to the margins or out of sight in the life of the community. No. Not at all. We are very visible and active. As prophets we speak the word of the Lord. We listen to stories and name how God is present. The spirit of wisdom rests on us as we identify what God is up to in our midst. The faith community blesses our ministry and holds our witness and speaking as a valuable and integral part of our life together.

When Paul came to visit our house church on his way to Jerusalem, our ministry was named and blessed—even by the visitors. In fact, while Paul was here, one of our male prophet friends Agabus visited and told how Paul would be bound if he went to Jerusalem. The community accepted his word and tried to convince Paul not to go on. Agabus's word—as ours—was and is respected.

But our story is longer and goes deeper. It really goes back to Jerusalem to those early days when the apostles were too busy with their teaching and prayers to attend to the needs of our gentile Christian folks. The apostles met to decide and delegated the selection process to the gentile community after laying down some preliminary requirements rooted in faith values. The stipulations for selecting leaders were (1) select seven from among yourselves (seven was a spiritually rich number signifying wholeness); (2) select persons who are in good standing; (3) select those who are full of the Spirit; (4) select those who are wise.

The apostles must have trusted that community because they did not try to control or manipulate the outcome. Of course, that decision laid a heavy burden on our father's friends to be discerning in their selection of leaders. Who was God calling for this ministry? Seven were chosen—all with Greek names—and our father, Philip, was one of them. The most famous was Stephen, a courageous and dynamic witness, who became the first Christian martyr, stoned for the truth of his preaching.

All seven leaders were set apart by the apostles through prayer and the laying on of hands—a good start for "apostolic succession." And it continued for us. Our father was an evangelist, and we joined him in the ministry. We were a family of those who spoke for God. The very fact that our house church and the network of house churches that comprised the faith community recognized our ministry was congruent with the inner testimony of the Spirit that we were called to leadership.

You may not have heard much about us. The written record of those times primarily recorded the work of male leaders. But like the two Marys and the other women around Jesus, we have been very visible in the leadership of the church. It feels like those apostolic hands laid upon our father were extended to us as well.

Today's authentic spiritual leaders attempt to focus on ways to connect with other people for a life-giving exchange of energy. In our work we hear that such leaders are open to inquiry and innovation. They value community, have respect for differences, and appreciate resilient forms of membership and organizing structures. Good spiritual leaders value permeable boundaries both within the congregation and beyond it. Authentic leaders regard spirituality as *the* potent source of life for ministry.

The requirements or expectations that a nominating committee names as criteria for leadership selection should be significantly rooted in the congregation's faith values. The following selection story from a United Methodist congregation in Ohio illustrates this point.

A WITNESS FROM A CONGREGATION
Ginghamsburg United Methodist Church, Dayton, Ohio

Ginghamsburg United Methodist Church, located in a small community north of Dayton, Ohio, is an unusual church.

Instead of reflecting the pattern of declining attendance in some mainline churches, it is a large, growing church that folks seek out because of its special spiritual DNA, marked by vital worship, group life, commitment, and lay ministries.

In an attempt to allow the leadership structure to fit the dynamic of the new life and ministry the church was experiencing, the usual leadership organization structure was reformed into a leadership core that could offer guidance and spiritual wisdom to the life of the congregation.

The administrative board, the board of trustees, as well as the personnel, nominations, and finance committees were replaced by a new *leadership board*. The new board would include nine to twelve lay leaders and six persons from the management staff. This new board would be given oversight of the body as a whole without being segmented into particular ministry areas. A primary condition for selection of board members was that each one be active in ministry.

For the transition, the existing administrative board designated a small group of selectors. Names of potential new board members were suggested to the selectors, and they began a screening process. They considered only church members. (Becoming a member required participation in a twelve-week class called "Vital Christianity.") The selection group began their work by conducting telephone interviews, asking the following questions: "Where does your current passion lie?" "What is your sense of call at this time?" "What do you see as the greatest need for our church and the community as well?"

Thirty persons were interviewed. The selectors then came together with their records and notes from the phone interviews. After prayerful consideration and sifting, the selection team invited twelve persons, each to come for a forty-five minute interview with the team. That interview focused on each person's spiritual formation and engagement in spiritual practices within the life of the church; for instance, celebration and worship, small group life, call to ministry—both within the church and outside of it—and participation in tithing. All the leaders were to come out of the church ministries. In the course of the interview the selectors asked many questions, including: "How would you describe the Ginghamsburg Church to someone else?" "How would you describe the pastor of the church to someone else?"

The selectors identified the final nine to twelve persons via prayer and discernment. They had committed to open dialogue with agreement to a common affirmation and consensus choices. They chose selectees for a three-year commitment to board leadership.

Commenting on the selection process after it was completed, then staff member Tammy Kelley said, "The selection process actually built community among the people, one group moving forward with a common goal and focus." Pastor Michael Slaughter observed, "We are now aligned for sharp, focused mission." And those selected, having experienced the process, said, "Because the process was extensive, we felt God's call to partner in leadership and are honored to have been chosen."

At least two authors, Max De Pree and Margaret Wheatley, suggest that effective leaders demonstrate an ability to improvise and also a readiness to make risky decisions. Effective leaders even see the value and appreciate the potential of periods of disequilibrium! In *Quantum Leaps: Seven Skills for Workplace ReCreation,* Charlotte Shelton recognizes the inadequacy of time-honed skills such as planning and organizing apart from skills that use both hemispheres of the brain. Given these kinds of insights on leadership from various disciplines, what qualities should selectors be looking for in potential leaders, and what questions should they be asking?

Some dioceses, presbyteries, and other church bodies offer handbooks and pamphlets listing suggested gifts or qualities for particular leadership roles. These descriptions are usually quite informative and helpful to local congregations. Unfortunately these publications often fail to remind selectors to look beyond the generic descriptions to the congregation-specific needs.

In the church, where members attempt to build up the temple of God, it is important to consider spiritual as well as other personal gifts as leadership candidates are identified. In many churches, members have not thought about spiritual gifts as relevant to selecting leaders!

People seeking leaders in various churches have shared the following statements about spiritual gifts with us. They reflect concern for gifts any selection committee might consider. (See chapter 5 for additional discussion of gift identification.)

- We are looking for persons who can articulate how they are authentically striving for holiness.
- We seek persons who believe in the integration of prayer with faith-full decision making.
- We need persons who love the church, who are able to express its mission to those within and those outside the church.
- We desire future-oriented leaders, men and women who take responsibility for listening to everyone.

Selectors often desire a combination of personal and spiritual gifts, as these statements illustrate:

- We search for persons who know how to question others carefully, who deal with conflict in constructive ways.
- We desire women and men who are aware of their strengths

and limitations, persons who will articulate them to us honestly in the process of discernment.

- We search for persons who believe that our congregation, with its human and material resources and its shortcomings, is held in a common trust.
- We desire men and women with focused energy, persons who can acknowledge and let go of their own agendas.
- We seek persons who have the desire and the time to give to this leadership role and who will commit wholeheartedly to engaging in it for the common good of the congregation.

Finding Potential Candidates and Gathering Information from Them

What sources of connection, introduction, or identification are available when a selection team is ready to create a pool of candidates? Are potential leaders to be found within the fold or via a national search?

Ellen's religious congregation invites all members to consider a leadership role within the community and to share understandings of their own potential leadership qualities within small groups of members. Then, over a period of three to four months, clusters of small groups meet to identify persons they want to encourage to enter into further discernment regarding a leadership position. Following this process, every member may send up to five invitations to individuals, encouraging them to participate in a discernment weekend for potential leaders (recipients of a significant number of invitations). The invitations are half-sheets of paper with this message: "I am inviting you to consider serving as _____ for the following reasons. . . ." Space for comments and the sender's signature follows.

Some nominating committees have a pool of potential candidates from the work of previous committees. Some local congregations engage in ongoing education/formation sessions regarding the role and ministry of church leaders, for example, using the book *Call to Leadership: Transforming the Local Church* (see Resources). During these sessions, potential leaders begin to surface because of their obvious interest in the topic. Or some congregations schedule town meetings or listening sessions to talk about leadership needs. However potential candidates surface, the *reasons* persons are suggested is at the heart of the matter. The following story gets at that heart.

A WITNESS FROM A DISCERNMENTARIAN
Maria Thornton McClain
Roman Catholic parish, Indiana

One person, an eighty-three-year-old man, told the persons attending a parish meeting that he didn't know why he had agreed to come to the meeting. He viewed himself as unworthy to be a member of the parish pastoral council because he didn't know how much he could give. He stated that he had colon cancer that had spread to his liver and lungs. After drawing out of him his belief that he did think he had something to contribute, he agreed to have his name listed as being interested.

The other council members, including the pastor, unanimously supported him, and said they would leave in God's hands how much time he would have to give and said his views would be welcomed. He had been on the council before and had a sense of what was really important for the parish.

What a gift he will be to the council! He also has been given a reason to live, a purpose for whatever time he has left.

He walked out of that meeting with renewed energy, wondering how he would tell this one to his wife.

❖

Think about how your selectors and candidates will engage in spiritual discernment once candidates begin to emerge. As in any experience of communal prayer, a comfortable space where the selectors and potential leaders can see and hear one another is an essential component. In meetings, generous time for a welcome and introductions followed by a significant period of vocal and silent prayer will set the tone for a working and learning community in its beginning stage.

From our experience of facilitating spiritual discernment processes with Roman Catholic parish pastoral council members, we understand how important it is for selectors to come to a shared commitment with one another regarding particular attitudes and behaviors. Initial agreement about attitudes and behavior within the group will provide a litmus test throughout a discernment process if for some reason dysfunctional or unhelpful behaviors begin to surface, such as losing patience over the time spent in so many meetings. Agreed-upon attitudes might include (1) an openness of heart and mind to listen carefully to others; (2) a willingness to keep oneself in a spirit of prayer, listening to the voices within and outside of oneself; (3) a demonstration of reverence for the wisdom everyone brings to the group; (4) a desire to relinquish the need to control, heal, or fix a person or process; and (5) a recognition of one's own gifts and a willingness to share these with the group.

Statements such as the following address individual and group behaviors: (1) We will consistently search for clarity of understanding, such as checking out our assumptions about what others say or do. (2) We will let others finish speaking before formulating a response. (3) We will strive to speak what we really think and be willing to clarify the meaning of our words when asked about them. (4) We will show that we value one another by expressing any needs or discomforts we observe as soon as they occur.

Another important conversation for your selection group and candidates at this point concerns the time commitment essential for spiritual discernment. Spiritual discernment happens more on God's timing than the neat time frames we often conform to, some of which can be imposed upon a selection committee by a national or regional governing body. With some groups we've agreed to schedule successive meetings only after each session is complete and when people have their calendars in hand. We've also agreed not to meet if everyone in the group cannot be present. We came to this particular decision because we felt that the group would be deprived of the pieces of wisdom from absent members.

Gathering information from each candidate is critical. You may start with a printed form, such as a profile sheet, or a face-to-face meeting, such as a Roman Catholic parish's education/formation session for council ministry. However you decide to implement it, be sure you engage in conversation around the history and ethos of the leadership body with each candidate. What elements or dimensions of the congregation's story do you need to share up front with the candidates? How will you invite candidates to tell some of their personal faith, life, and career story? Selectors need information of substance, not substantial information, about a person's gifts and calling in order to weave the congregational and personal stories together.

In a prayerful, trusting environment selectors can encourage conversation about the values the candidates hold, their motivations, their greatest strengths, even some of their limitations. Here are sample questions you might use:

- What challenges have you had to face?
- What models of governance have you experienced?
- Have you experienced working as a team player, and what was that like for you?
- How do you define *leadership*?
- What motivates you?
- How do you define the capacity to *think big*?
- To what degree do you think that capacity is yours?
- Who has ministered to you? Describe the personal and professional qualities of this person.

Selectors shouldn't forget the spirituality questions:

- Have you ever experienced the impossible becoming possible? What happened?
- What part of your life do you know as God's handiwork?
- Tell us about your sense of the church as community.
- What does the language of the cross have to do with your life?
- What valuable gift has God entrusted to you?
- How important is scripture to you, and how are the scriptures being fulfilled in your life today?
- Do you see yourself as a servant? How?
- How do you deal with failure?
- For what grace do you regularly pray?

If candidates know the local congregation well, selectors may ask questions like these:

- What would you like to see happen in this congregation in the next three to five years?
- Where do you see this congregation at the edge of new growth?
- Where is the congregation struggling? Where is it stuck?

By asking such questions, selectors become more aware of the various gifts and skills among the potential leaders. Of course, interviewing candidates is not complete until you ask, "What questions do you have for us?" The potential leaders themselves begin to look for complementary gifts in ways that help focus the selectors' continuing discernment.

Selectors corporately discern the best combination of gifts in response to a congregation's leadership needs. At the same time, they affirm every candidate's personal call to ministry, whether the selectors discern a particular leadership role at this time or in a ministry yet to be discovered. The habit and practice of spiritual discernment acknowledge that everyone has received gifts from God. Selection by discernment does not produce winners and losers.

Selectors then need to help one another become attuned to strange twists or surprising coincidences they may experience along the way of discernment. They need carefully to avoid the human tendency of making people fit an initial perception. They may ask one another for help when they feel uncentered or wonder if what they're hearing is somewhat distorted.

Selectors are a learning group stirring after God's desire. Selectors are a praying group looking for that shared vision in service of the common good. Their experience may be messy, but the call is to be faithful to the work of God's spirit.

The story of Esther's selection as queen is a messy one, indeed, but some good came out of it all.

from Esther, a Selectee

(based on the Book of Esther)

My life has been one of which fairy tales are made. I was born a Jewish commoner, then had the misfortune of being orphaned at an early age. When that happened I went to live with my cousin Mordecai, who eventually adopted me and raised me as his daughter.

During my teen years an unfortunate occurrence took place. At the time I wasn't sure how the event would affect me, but it certainly has in surprising ways. King Ahasuerus, who ruled many provinces from India to Ethiopia, became angry with Queen Vashti because she refused to come before him at his command. He banished her from the palace, removed her title, and took away her luxurious lifestyle. (Many women continue to see her as a role model, however, because she had the courage to resist domination by her spouse.)

After Queen Vashti was banished, the king sought to name another queen, and I was chosen from among many beautiful young women. Now I am sure the king selected me on the basis of my good looks, not the political savvy or other skills that began to surface as a result of my selection as queen.

While I was still rather new at being queen, my cousin discovered a conspiracy against the king's life and asked me to reveal this to Ahasuerus. I did, and that's when I began to find myself in the midst of trouble. As one event led to another, I discovered myself in a leadership position that would allow me to assist my Jewish people in a time of real crisis, though technically I had no authority or power. I was royalty in name only.

Here's what happened. The king's highest official, Haman, decreed that all the Jews in the kingdom should be killed. To make this long story short, Haman's life was taken in place of my cousin Mordecai's, whom Haman had intended to kill. The outcome precipitated more violence than I like to acknowledge, but through my intercession with the king, my kinfolk were granted permission to defend themselves by killing those who would have killed them. I was able to use my favor with the king to intercede for my people's welfare during this difficult and violent time.

My selection as queen might not have come about through the perfect process, but God used me to bring clarity and comfort to my kinfolk.

❖

4

WEIGHING OPTIONS

We mentioned earlier that congregations are held together by values, beliefs, and foundational stories. During the weighing movement, selectors need to rely on these strong congregational threads because they sustain the passion to move the group forward in spiritual discernment.

The movement of *weighing* sorts and tests options in response to the leading of God's Spirit. During the time of weighing options, selectors still need spiritual vision to see *through* each of the options, to inspect every facet or detail with the mind's eye. Selectors are looking *into* each option, carefully examining each one for its best possibilities. Selectors are attempting to see each option clearly despite "spirits" other than God's that lurk among a group, such as the spirit of impatience or the spirit of seeking harmony at any cost.

Selectors weigh capabilities, skills, gifts, motivations (as best they are known), past and present behaviors related to a particular leadership role, and the differences in these factors among the candidates. In other words, selectors weigh all the criteria established before the selection process began—in both head and heart. "God, who would you have us select to lead the church at this time?" In addition, selectors in spiritual discernment are looking not only for deep truths but also for illusions held by group members and prospective leaders. "Beloved, do not believe every spirit, but test the spirits to see whether they are from God" (1 John 4:1). Now allow the Apostle Paul, from his vantage point as a selectee, to share what he learned about selecting leaders for the church.

A BIBLICAL WITNESS

from Paul, a Selectee
(based on Acts 9; 11)

The story of my conversion is well known. That dramatic episode on the road to Damascus—a flash of light from heaven and the audible voice of Jesus (heard by my companions as well)—has become the folklore of many a Sunday school classroom. But my selection and preparation as a leader in witness and ministry are not as well known, so let me tell you about those experiences.

After that dramatic encounter with the spirit of Jesus on the Damascus road, my friends led me by the hand into the city. I was stunned, couldn't see anything, was bewildered, and couldn't make much sense of my experience. I did the only thing that I knew. I prayed— prayers like "Lord, have mercy on me, a sinner. What are you doing in my life? Help me see." I was confused and everything seemed chaotic. I'm not sure I knew the extent of change and redirection that would be called for—except that suffering would be involved. (After all, precipitating suffering had been my business!)

I had to sort things out and come to some clarity about my new identity in Christ and the new purpose that he had in mind for me. Just when a vision revealed that I would have a visitor, a man named Ananias showed up at the door. He came with fear and trembling, thinking that this situation might be a trap. But God's spirit compelled him to cross that boundary of fear and come to me. He laid hands on me, prayed for me, and baptized me. Suddenly I could see. When we sat down to eat together to discuss all that had happened, Ananias asked me to consider being a witness to the gentile world, even to rulers and kings. Somehow God had impressed on his heart a vision of God's choosing me for this task. I was overwhelmed, yet I could begin to see my calling take shape as we continued to pray and reflect together over those next days.

Twice I had to run for my life after initial steps to witness in Damascus and later in Jerusalem. Each time my new Christian friends protected me, and they finally sent me off to Tarsus. After their embrace of my faith and inner calling, I had a good long spell in the desert, so to speak. There I was more fully formed and grounded.

Eventually another great spiritual leader, Barnabas, a leader in the church in Jerusalem, selected me to assist in Antioch, where we had a productive ministry with a large group of new believers. Folks there began calling us "Christians."

From many conversations with Ananias and Barnabas I learned several truths about selecting leaders for the church. Whoever is selected needs to be well formed and grounded in faith in Jesus. And, the task of those who select is to discern if, where, and how God is already shaping a call in someone's life. They ask themselves, "Whom is God already calling for this specific ministry?" The choice may not be immediately obvious. At least I was not an obvious choice! But praise God for the courage, patience, intuition, and vision of the Christians who surrounded me!

The importance of sorting things out and coming to clarity of identity in Christ is affirmed in Luke Timothy Johnson's book *Scripture and Discernment: Decision Making in the Church.* Johnson writes that without processing the narrative of our experience of God, spiritual discernment never begins; without such processing, decisions can be theologically counterfeit.

In the weighing movement, selectors help the candidates name leadership gifts they might put at the service of the church community. They assist the candidates in describing their limitations, or, worded in a more positive way, the qualities and skills needed in other persons to complement their own gifts. All the while selectors look for complementary gifts in the "holy collection" of persons. No possibility should ever be overlooked.

This fanciful tale illustrates what can happen when we're involved in spiritual weighing. A water bearer in India had two large pots that hung on opposite ends of the pole he carried across his neck daily. One pot was perfect; the other had a small crack in it. For two years the perfect pot always delivered a full portion of water to the house of his master, while the cracked pot arrived only half full.

Of course the perfect pot was proud of its accomplishments, while the cracked one was ashamed of its imperfection. One afternoon the deficient pot decided to speak to the water bearer. It said, "I am ashamed of myself, and I need to apologize to you." "Why, and what for?" asked the water bearer. "I have been able to deliver only half my load because this crack in my side causes water to leak out," replied the pot.

The water bearer felt sorry for the imperfect pot and told it, "As I walk back to the master's house I want you to notice the beautiful flowers along the side of the road." As the water bearer climbed the hill, the imperfect pot took notice of the sun warming the beautiful wildflowers beside the road. But at the end of the walk the pot still felt bad because it had leaked out half its load. Sensing its feelings, the water bearer said to the pot, "Didn't you notice that there were flowers only on your side of the road? That's because I have always known about your flaw, and I have taken advantage of it. I planted flower seeds on your side of the road, and every day while I walk back from the stream, you give them a nice drink of water. Without your being just the way you are, we would not be able to see these beautiful flowers alongside the road."

In God's great economy our flaws or limitations are compensated by the gifts and skills of others. Many congregations are wonderfully diverse spiritually, culturally, racially, theologically, and economically, and this diversity begs for calling forth a variety of gifts. How do selectors creatively and carefully weigh the variety of gifts? They may turn to silence now and then—a silence that offers respite from the flood of words and the reams of paper selection committees tend to collect. Silence helps people to attend to what is happening "now," restoring inner resources, empowering a more intent listening to God's word, and allowing space to ponder the words. Silence can validate an experience or cause movement beyond the moment.

Selectors might find these questions helpful as they engage in weighing:

- Do I/we need more specific conversation about _____?
- What has not yet happened that I/we would like to see happen?
- Is there something I/we are reluctant to name aloud that should be shared?

During this movement selectors might ask candidates to respond to questions about hypothetical scenarios. Inviting the candidates to acknowledge critical insights about themselves in relationship to one another (if the candidates are meeting with selectors as a group), or in relationship to church leaders, would add new insights at this time.

Maria Thornton McClain, a discernmentarian, shares one of her experiences, facilitating a process for selecting school commission members.

A WITNESS FROM A
ROMAN CATHOLIC PARISH
Maria Thornton McClain

Recently a Roman Catholic church contracted with me to lead a group in discerning new members. I had conducted discernment of members for groups in this parish before and knew something about the parish's culture.

The first group I met with was the school commission. On the evening of the discernment seven people whose names had been submitted showed up, as well as the pastor and an officer of the commission. Two of the seven would be discerned as members of the commission. We met in a room in the church building where I welcomed them, explained the rhythm of our time together, and led them in introducing themselves and completing the sentence "Something you don't know about me is. . . ."

The commission representative led the group into the church, placed a candle representing Christ on the altar, and lit it. I led the group in a reflection on "The Call of Samuel" and their call, coming from God and affirmed by the community. Then each one wrote on a small piece of paper a talent or ability each would bring to the commission. I told the group members that no one would see what they wrote. They walked to the altar and placed the paper in a basket next to the lit candle. They then wrote down something they felt they were holding too closely and needed to let go—maybe a sense of unworthiness or a sense of obligation to assure that the commission would deal with a certain concern. I reminded them that no one would see what they wrote. They placed these papers in the basket on the altar. I told them that we would continue our prayer in the meeting room. Carrying the lit candle, the commission representative led the group to the room.

When everyone reached the room, we placed the candle and a Bible on a table in the center of the group. I asked the candidates to tell us, from their experience in the parish, what they understood about discernment. I could hear from their responses that the concept and practice of discernment really had taken hold in the parish. I expanded their notions in a brief presentation on the meaning of discernment in the Christian tradition.

The next step was for the commission representative and pastor to explain the mission of the parish and its school, the role of the school commission, and how the pastor interacted with the group. The pastor, a Benedictine monk, related how Saint Benedict had told the monks that it would behoove an abbot to seek the views of each and every member of the community, even the very youngest, before making a decision. The commission representative explained the expectations of individual members and the support new members receive from the group.

After a short discussion, I asked everyone to spend some time in silence, listening to hear whether each still were called to this ministry. All said yes. We then had another period of silence for each one to prepare his or her responses to three questions: (1) What abilities would you bring to the commission? (2) Why do you feel you can fulfill the expectations of members? and (3) What one thing would be difficult for you as a member of the commission, for which you would ask the group's help? All told the group their answers, and each person in turn answered clarifying questions.

Another period of silence followed. During this time all members of the group prepared to state the name of someone in the group, other than themselves, they sensed was called to this ministry and to tell that person why. Next, they named another person (which could be themselves) who they believed was so called. After going around the room a few times, there was a three-way tie, and it seemed the group was not ready to go further. The commission representative, the pastor, and I already had agreed that if something like this were to happen, the process would be continued by the whole school commission at a special meeting. If the tie persisted, the commission members would put the names in a hat and draw for the selectee, remembering that the apostles chose someone to replace Judas by the same method.

Well, guess what? At the school commission meeting a few days later, after each of the three prospective members answered the same questions and then left the room, the commission members stated the name of one person they felt was called to this ministry and why. After silent prayer each one wrote the name of one person. One person was supported by two-thirds of the group. When they repeated the process with the two remaining names, there was a tie. Yes, they put both names in a hat and drew one out. The three prospective members were brought back in and told who had been chosen. In all, the process was peaceful and prayerful.

I thank God for the pastor and the style of leadership he has brought to the parish, one that encourages discerning where the Holy Spirit is leading in all major decisions. Without such a leader discernment could not happen!

After much research, perhaps many interviews, lots of prayer, silence, and conversation, and after repeated listening for indications toward agreement on a candidate(s), selectors attempt to reach closure and a time of *resting* (another movement) on their selection. Selectors may now begin to see God's yearning associated with a particular candidate or a particular combination of candidates who possess special gifts for transformational leadership within the congregation. These candidates are highly motivated by the congregation's story and deeply envision the spiritual significance and particular demands of its leadership, in other words, congregational growth and actualization.

Selectors may now find themselves resonating more and more with the text from Acts: "It seems good to the Holy Spirit and to us." And selectors may find themselves reflecting on the wholesome difference between a spiritual discernment selection process and previous selection processes in which they were invested in particular candidates' "winning."

On the other hand, unfortunately, selectors may find themselves at an impasse regarding the persons or the configuration of persons who should be selected at the time of the *closing* movement. Selectors may find themselves experiencing varying degrees of conflict arising from polarities that have surfaced. What were once considered common understandings may no longer seem clear or adequate. Negative feelings about one another or discomfort about the process may have sprung up. For example, some selectors may want to challenge and question old standards that have been in place "forever," by introducing "new blood," while others may want to preserve the status quo by selecting "safe people."

Differences of opinion or hesitations to agree actually may help rather than hinder a discernment process. Sometimes reflecting on a fantasy such as *Aria da Capo: A Play in One Act* by Edna St. Vincent Millay is helpful when selectors are "stuck." That story goes something like this: Two shepherds are sitting together in a field watching their sheep. Being rather bored, one of them suggests that they play a game of gathering rocks and building a wall—a wall between them. They work out some of the rules, such as, neither can go to the other's side without permission, and they begin gathering the stones to build the wall. After they build a very fine wall, they agree to sit by themselves for a while and figure out a plot wherein they might outdo each other. Then one shepherd finds that there is a stream on his side of the wall, so he enjoys a good drink from it. Would he give the other shepherd a drink? No.

Some time later the other shepherd shouts that he has gold on his side of the wall. Can the other shepherd have some? Of course not, because what's on his side belongs to him. Could he trade some water for some gold? No, because what's over there belongs to the other and what's over here belongs to him. Each shepherd wishes for what the other has but is unwilling to give up his own treasure.

When one of the shepherds suggests taking the wall down, the other agrees. But when they attempt to remove the stones, the stones won't move! The more the shepherds pull and tug, the angrier they become with the wall and with each other. As the story continues, each one reaches over the wall to choke the other. And as the story ends, each shepherd falls dead into the other's field.

We know aspects of this story well because we see it every day in the political lives of our world and our nation. We know too that the church's story differs from the world's story. We know God yearns for disciples to demonstrate a more excellent way.

Reflecting on scripture again may help bring God's ways and the selectors' human ways into congruence. Scripture, taken to heart, touches a deep core and stirs God-given creativity. Consider the story of the Council of Jerusalem (Acts 15), noticing the love the apostles and elders shared and the high value they placed on unity through-out their deliberations. The Letter to the Ephesians explains to new gentile converts that the blood of Christ "has broken down the divid-ing wall, that is, the hostility between us . . . , thus making peace." In Christ, "the whole structure is joined together and grows into a holy temple in the Lord; in whom you also are built together spiritually into a dwelling place for God" (Eph. 2:13-22). Selectors too can pray for unity of mind and heart, for a groundswell of grace that will thaw differences of opinion and leave room to walk spiritually abreast of one another.

Selectors may need to plan additional time together, specifical-ly for the purpose of coming to agreement again. They may need to revisit their covenant to work until they have discovered what is good for all, to listen carefully to one another in order to better understand what each is saying, and always to test and confirm what each per-son is hearing.

The following story illustrates what can happen when members of a selection group relinquish personal preferences.

WITNESS FROM A
RELIGIOUS COMMUNITY
Mary Benet McKinney, OSB, Chicago, Illinois

I hold as precious countless experiences in many arenas of church life, but one stands out. That experience happened in a chapter meeting I facilitated with about two hundred Franciscan sisters.

I have a special devotion to the daily scripture readings assigned by the Roman Church and begin each day that I am working with a group by sharing a reflection based on those passages. This practice resulted in the following experience.

The goal of the women in this chapter meeting was to discern new community leadership. Like so many religious communities today, the elderly outnumbered the middle-aged and the young. In discerning a preferred future, the group had agreed that this point in their history called for new ideas and the courage to risk new approaches both to their ministries and to their lives together. But translating this decision into choices for leadership created some real fear, especially for the elderly.

For the past six years the sister responsible for health care in the community had done an outstanding job. She was compassionate and efficient. She created a safe and happy environment for the elderly sisters. They loved and trusted her. However, by nature, she was not a risk taker and not particularly creative in areas unrelated to care of the elderly. As the discerning process continued, five potential leaders emerged. She was one of them. The other four fit the profile called for by the defined future direction. After much discussion and prayer we did the first consensus test. Predictably the majority of the sisters, who felt safe with their beloved caregiver, chose her, so the balance was tipped in her favor.

That moment was very painful. The younger group saw their dreams of a more creative future about to be shattered. The elderly sisters, try as they might, could not quite understand the sadness that fell over the group.

What should be done? It was almost time for evening prayer, so I recommended that we go to prayer and supper and then spend the rest of the night in silence and prayerful reflection. I was not at all sure of the group's next step, but the next morning brought the answer!

The scripture reading for the day was from the Acts of the

Apostles, chapter 6. The Hellenists had complained that their widows were being overlooked in the daily distribution of food. So a meeting was called, and the twelve apostles addressed the group: "It is not right that we should neglect the word of God in order to wait on tables" (6:2). As a result of this meeting, people were designated to care for the needs of the community so that the Twelve could be about the word.

Having begun our morning session with this reading, the group discussed its implications for them. It became evident that the scripture was calling them to look to their leaders to lead, not just to be caregivers. Obviously those leaders would be responsible to assign others to do the caregiving. After spending time in private reflection, we came together again and talked about the implications of this insight. And that is when it happened!

One of the younger, dynamic women in the community stood and asked: "Widows! Why do you doubt that we would care for you? You have formed us, built the community we now are. We love you and respect you. What do you fear?"

For starters, the elders of the community had never been called widows before, so that created quite a stir. But the shoe fit and we all knew it! The discussion that followed was nothing short of the Spirit's speaking in and through the group. This conversation became the turning point in the discernment.

Ultimately a wise, prayerful, creative risk taker was discerned for the leadership position. And that is not the end of the story. The new leader and her council soon appointed the much-loved caregiver to continue in her position in the health care of the community.

In our small survey we discovered that most selection processes culminate in a written vote. If prayer and scripture do take place during the closing movement, it is usually at the request of the discernmentarian, moderator, or chairperson of the group. Because denominational polity may determine how selectors officially name and record the selection of leaders, we encourage selectors to think creatively about how they may integrate meaningful worship into the closing movement. We caution against an artificial spiritualization of the closing and resting movements in spiritual discernment. Here are some possible ways to incorporate a worshipful element in the closing movement:

- Recognize the gifts of each person who has participated in the selection process. All group members have self-disclosed some of their values and dreams and given of their time to the process.
- Reflect on 1 Corinthians 12:12-31 in conversation and prayer, then take turns highlighting the gifts of each group member.
- Offer blessing prayers for each participant.
- Present each person a special card with personalized words of thanksgiving.
- Choose a hymn, psalm, or piece of artwork that affirms everyone involved in the discernment as a focus for worship.

We all know that there is great wisdom in the biblical concept of Sabbath as a "day of rest for the heart." A selection committee needs just that—rest for the heart. When we let the land of our heart lie fallow that we are open to the *test of the heart* in spiritual discernment: Is there consolation or desolation in the choice or decision?

Think about the heart for a moment. Even when diseased, the heart is the strongest muscle in the body. Among the many images of the heart in scripture are: hearts of flesh and hearts of stone; steadfast and faint hearts; willing and troubled hearts; hearts of integrity; tender, pure, and wise hearts; glad hearts; and hearts that melt like wax.

Today's spiritual leaders need to be familiar with their own hearts. Can each leader characterize his or her heart? Perhaps it is courageous, stout but pliable in the face of challenges, strong enough to hear criticism without withering, forgiving, capable of enduring pain and relishing praise. We need spiritual leaders whose hearts evoke in us the importance of uniting mind and spirit, of striving side by side, and of living in a manner worthy of the body of Christ.

Selectors, with their collective heart, must experience *consolation* regarding their choice of a leader or leaders. Characteristics of this sense of consolation include a loss of worry about the choice, frequent episodes of appreciation for the person(s) they've selected, a sense of deep vitality and energy about the life and mission of the church. Their feeling about the selectee(s) is in tune with the scripture "'Let days speak, / and many years teach wisdom.' / But truly it is the spirit in a mortal, / the breath of the Almighty, that makes for understanding" (Job 32:7-8). Selectors experiencing consolation perceive a positive framework for future relationships and commitments between selectors and the chosen leadership, even though differing points of view might exist.

A story from Fairfax Unity Church in Oakton, Virginia, illustrates a discernment process rich in prayer, symbol, and a spirit of consolation. Eileen Goor and Amy Hagood of Discernment Ministry, New World Unity Church, Springfield, Virginia, were the discernment team facilitating the group. They have adopted the movements described in *Discerning God's Will Together* and nurtured them, as Eileen Goor says, "in the soil of Unity principles, watered them with our love, and focused attention until they germinated into a very exciting process we call Participating in God's Unfolding." Different terms and variations on the movements are evident, but the spirit of spiritual discernment is at the heart of the process.

A WITNESS FROM A
CHURCH BOARD

Eileen Goor

A board member from Fairfax Unity Church in Oakton, Virginia, requested that we [Goor and Hagood] facilitate a discernment process for the congregation to choose their new minister from a field of three qualified candidates. We readily accepted the opportunity to explore the effectiveness of the process and, in spite of natural apprehension in the face of the unknown, the church board agreed to enter into the adventure. The board members also allowed us to bring two "observers" who had a particular interest in the process. As it turned out, the observers' presence opened up whole new horizons for the process by prompting us to realize that at least two roles besides discernmentarian are vital elements in its success. The following account explains how the roles of *scribe* and *keeper of the flame* emerged.

When we arrived on a Tuesday evening, the room was arranged as usual for the board meeting: chairs around a rectangular table. We decided to assert the importance of having no obstructions, so the table came down and an open circle was formed with the chart board at one end. There was some resistance to the change since the table had held a candle and flowers and probably provided a measure of safety people were not aware of desiring. Someone mentioned taking a vote, and dodging darting glances, we responded that no votes would be taken that night.

After the opening prayer, a routine check-in procedure followed. This time, the check-in included voicing any concerns or hesitations people had about the process. The length of time the process might take was a common concern since the possibility of completing twelve movements in a reasonable amount of time (preferably by 10:00 P.M.) seemed questionable. We felt some unspoken tension about our rearrangement of the environment, and the energy seemed quite dispersed, but everyone agreed to continue. At that point, we asked a question fundamental to the authenticity of the process: "Are you open to the possibility that you could conclude none of the current candidates are God's idea for you?" We explained that without this level of openness, we would be limiting God to choosing between A and B, when our greatest good might be a total surprise. They agreed to this assumption. I believe our excitement, enthusiasm, and confident glow encouraged their trust.

Once we began the movements, we discovered immediately the need for a *scribe*. The discernmentarian, who facilitates the process, needs to focus on the participants and all of the elements that promote an effective process— observing when energy shifts call for returning to listening, noting when it is time to move on, reminding participants of their commitment to stay in the process (rather than revert to past behaviors).

Other demands of the process called for very different skills. The scribe's role calls for the ability to listen to an individual's comments and compress them into a few words that accurately reflect the intention of the speaker. Sometimes people throw out several comments in a row, and the scribe needs to hold them all in mind. As Spirit would have it, one of the observers who came with us had excellent skills in this vein and became the group's scribe.

Scribe in place, we proceeded with a short *listening* time to get centered. We keep all listening times to three or four minutes, so people don't leave their heart and start analyzing responses from an ego framework. We had learned from experience not to belabor a question. When we moved into *shaping*, we asked participants to respond with a question that simply would move them forward in the process. We emphasized the importance of crafting a question that begins with *What* because we recognize that the *Why* and *How* are up to God. We were careful not to lead the group in a specific direction even if members thought they knew exactly what question they would ask. We did not try to come up with specific wording for a single question. We encouraged them to consider where they really wanted to go rather than where they thought they wanted to go. Tension in the room still conveyed the impression of thoughts like *I don't see how this is going to get us a minister!* Members displayed a lot of closed-body language. We asked them if they felt any one of the questions offered could possibly lead to the desired result. Tentatively they agreed that one of the questions could lead to results, so we posted the list of questions. It took a great leap of faith to move out of the *shaping* movement to the next stage while feeling unsettled about how their efforts so far would get them where they wanted to be. At that point their desire was probably closer to *Let's just take a vote and get this thing over with!* than *Wow! It is exciting to see what God has in store for us!* Knowing this energy would change, we moved right along to *aligning*.

Aligning asks participants to list the guiding principles that underlie their decision making. What shared values can be stated that will assure everyone is coming from the same basic belief system? Can the group look to its vision statement or commonly held beliefs? Working through this movement generally loosens people up. The work empowers them to see the foundation of who they are together and how they serve. This experience fosters their recognition of community and the importance of a shared value system. At this stage in the Fairfax Unity group, body language began to change, and we saw smiles and laughter. When one of the self-identified hesitators listed "trust the process" as a shared value, we knew the group was on its way to a gratifying experience. People started to express the true self that each person must recognize in order to reveal God's plan for the group, and resistance seemed to melt away. Only the person in this group who was also on the search committee still seemed to have reservation. Someone in this position probably has worked on the task at hand with others for many months and senses a higher stake in the final outcome. Great faith allows a person to let go of all that work and trust the process of discernment.

The *releasing* movement flowed easily, openly, and quickly. Board members discussed both positive and negative experiences from past selection processes and their expectations for this process. At this juncture in spiritual discernment we usually interject a song called "I Release and I Let Go." The chorus ends, "I am only here for God." We sing that a couple of times, then rest in this energy. Inevitably people are truly able to release their anxiety and preconceived notions of how this is all "supposed to work." Everyone stands up and shakes out the stiffness from sitting. Releasing is a great discovery experience. People can bring their fears and reservations out in the open.

We used to call our next movement *becoming*, but we realized that its purpose is stepping into the truth of who we are. A better name is *proclaiming*. The Fairfax group had a great time proclaiming. Proclaiming is generally done simply, naming single words to describe spiritual insights. It is a unifying and genuine experience, and some people choose to become vulnerable at this point. Once the group sees how much everyone has to offer and the immensity of their potential, they realize the results of the process may be greater than any of them had imagined.

The *contributing* movement asks individuals to state what gifts each is willing to offer to this situation. We remind them they are speaking for themselves here and not for a neighbor or the group in general. This movement is very valuable later when implementation is discussed. When participants make this commitment of gifts in the flow of enlarging their picture of themselves further affirms the potential for accomplishing more than previously expected.

After the contributing movement comes a natural break time when participants can bask in all they have accomplished. When they return, singing helps to reestablish the bond they have formed. Next we ask, "Can you choose the question that will lead you forward? The wording is important. Does it fit who you are, what you are, and what you want to accomplish? Is it specific enough? Or is it too broad?" The Fairfax group experienced some confusion at this point, so we went back to listening. More often than not with listening, the question drops into the midst of the group like a penny dropping onto the sidewalk, heads up and shiny! That was the case for the Fairfax board. One person stated a new question (quite simple and aligned with the guiding principles). The question reflected the energy of the previous list of questions, and everyone agreed immediately that this question could take them forward.

Once everyone agreed on the question, we moved right into *anchoring*—to anchor their current feeling in an image, fable, song, history, or scripture text. In this case, "Surely the presence of the Lord is in this place" was perfect. The group also embraced the story of Solomon's choosing a discerning heart and receiving all of God's abundance in response.

We proceeded on to *seeking*. The discernmentarian asked the question that had been formulated, and after three or four minutes of silence, the telling moment was palpable in the room. Each person received an answer in a different mode, but each response clearly pointed to the same choice for new ministers: Donna and Terry Dearmore. One person heard the name Dearmore; another saw Terry's face. One person heard the complement of biblical teachings the congregation had identified as vital for their new ministers. Another person saw the image of a deer running across a grassy field and was delighted to realize the connection to the Dearmores. Yet another person heard a particular teaching from the Sunday service. All realized they were of one mind, and their answer was clear. The Dearmores were intended for the spiritual leadership of Unity in Fairfax. Obviously it would be easy to deliver this news to the congregation.

Since only one option was considered, we moved right into *expanding*, discovering what the option would look like expanded to its highest and best. The whole group became extremely animated, galloping through possibilities that amplified its revelation. Group members supported one another as they envisioned and enlarged the vision with each additional comment. Their vision depicted the effects they wanted to bring forth in their church. This celebration was awe-inspiring!

Converging calls for restating the option clearly and concisely so all are confident they are in agreement. It also includes two questions used to assure that the conclusion is expansive enough: "Is it good for all? Is it awesome enough for God to have room to move?" By the time we reached this juncture in the process, the answers to these questions came swiftly. Yes and yes! Had there been any hesitation at this point, we would have returned to some of the earlier movements. But in this instance, there was no uncertainty.

At this point, the discernmentarian slipped out of the process and asked the chaos-producing question "What do you want to do now?" For the next five minutes everyone began speaking at once. For the first time all night people walked on one another's comments, interrupted or reacted rather than responded. Fortunately the discernmentarian realized what had transpired and asked for a time of listening. The group was then able to agree on the conditions of *resting*.

When the group reconvened two nights later, the members moved into shaping an entirely new question related to what they would offer the new ministers. After releasing all outdated thoughts about limitations and proclaiming the truth of what they had to offer, each person listed the gifts he or she would contribute. They then listened to Spirit, seeking the option God would have them offer the Dearmores. The option was to invite the Dearmores to a weekend retreat, and the group asked us to return to facilitate a day of discernment related to the Dearmores' contract (which on that day transformed into a covenant). When some doubts arose concerning the viability of this decision, the group promptly dispelled them with the understanding that what Spirit had arranged would flow beautifully and "from this trust, all else grows."

The *implementation* movement included extending this invitation to the Dearmores (which they readily accepted), calling the other candidates to let them know of the decision (we're told that they received the news graciously), and reporting to the congregation. The energy of the process was conveyed to the congregation in such a way that all are clear the church will never be the same again. Our work helped bring about a willingness to "Participate in God's Unfolding."

The hidden presence of God's Spirit became visible in the selection of the Dearmores for pastoral leadership, and the spiritual relationship between New World Unity Church and Fairfax Unity Church continues. A few months after this selection process concluded, New World invited a discernment team from Fairfax to facilitate a discernment for their church.

A nominating committee will find that its usual ways of describing successful decision making no longer apply when it uses the movements of spiritual discernment as articulated in *Discerning God's Will Together* or a denomination-specific translation of the movements (such as the Unity translation called "Participating in God's Unfolding" or the United Methodists' *Seeking and Doing God's Will: Discernment for the Community of Faith*, which uses the Wesleyan quadrilateral as its framework). The practice of spiritual discernment frees selectors to venture into the awesome territory of *seeking God's yearning*, and so the process may leave them with the challenge of not knowing enough about God's work to really evaluate it! Yet in the end, if selectors trust that whenever two, three, or more are gathered to prayerfully uncover God's yearning for the church, they will know that they entered into a sacred space within which the Spirit of God fed and led the process.

5

GIFTS DIFFERING

Outside the realm of spiritual discernment, background, pedigree, ambition, wealth, social status, and power often play important, if unacknowledged, roles in selecting persons for leadership positions. Gift identification is an important component in the selection of church leaders, especially when spiritual gifts of God's Spirit are considered; for example, a habit and practice of prayer, a sensitivity to how God is working in one's own life. While personal gifts are important, in the final analysis they are not the conclusive determinants of church leaders. We know from experience that even the best efforts to match the gifts of a candidate with the needs of a particular congregation will not necessarily guarantee a good—never mind perfect—match. In fact, chairpersons of selection committees who have become disillusioned with their choices report that intensive matchmaking can produce disastrous results. So, for the purpose of this book, we want to look deeper into the heart of the matter of gifts differing.

Hearing God's Call

Congregations that are intentional about pursuing a life of the "Spirit" and the "us" usually focus on mission, gather and govern in flexible ways, and value their network of relationships. Selection committees in these congregations endeavor to avoid requiring selectees for leadership to fit into narrow categories but rather keep an eye out for a diversity of gifts and experiences. What these selectors primarily look for in potential candidates is the ability to intentionally connect "God's call" and "God's gift" in their own lives.

The witness of biblical accounts tells us that a "call" is initiated by God. Perhaps many persons are involved in the instigation of a call, but an authentic call to ministry is not vigorously sought by the individual being called. Elements of mystery accompany each call. And we realize (most often in hindsight) that God's timing of a call is significant.

A call to ministry may come in the midst of pain. A call may be motivated by a vision of how "things can be different." A call may trigger feelings of resistance or acceptance, but these feelings do not initially, or even finally, determine the validity of God's call. God is present in and around the call. And an authentic call by God will be validated by the faith community for whom the call is activated. Let's consider the call Nehemiah received to rebuild the wall of Jerusalem, putting his call to the test of these understandings of authenticity.

A BIBLICAL WITNESS

from Nehemiah, a Selectee
(based on Nehemiah 1:1–6:15)

My spirit has always been able to empathize with people undergoing great difficulties. I also have a heart for resolving environmental issues for the benefit of the earth. Those passions seemed to prompt me to ask my brother, Hanani, about the Jews who had escaped and survived and about the city of Jerusalem itself. What I heard in his firsthand account greatly saddened and perplexed me.

I learned that the survivors were experiencing many physical difficulties as well as devastating shame, both personal and communal, and that the city was in rubble after the fire. This news set me on a course of prayer—one of deep confession and lament for all I and my family had failed to do to keep the commandments given to Moses. But this knowledge also set me on a course of physical action, one for which I hardly seemed prepared. (And, I already had enough to do as cupbearer to the king!) In my heart I felt compelled to change this intolerable situation for the better.

My employer and trusted friend, King Artaxerxes, was a mentor and enabler to me. He asked pivotal questions to help me discern how I might respond to the situation, and he was especially attuned to my spirit. My spirit truly sought God's leading in what seemed to be an insurmountable task: bringing together that particular Jewish community and their environment—physically and spiritually—in order for them to deepen their relationship with God and for the glory of God.

The king gave me letters to guarantee my safe passage until I arrived in Judah, and to my astonishment he even directed the keeper of the forest to give me timber. He sent army officers with me, and over time King Artaxerxes mustered all the material support he could to help me. This support was very affirming because Sanballat the Horonite, Tobiah the Ammonite official, and Geshem the Arab gave me more than a little trouble, including threats on my life and the lives of those cooperating with me. Throughout these trials, I was always able to say openly and sincerely what I believed: "The God of heaven is the one who will give us success" (Neh. 2:20).

The Jewish people who collaborated with me were a motley yet holy crew of goldsmiths, perfume makers, servants, merchants, a few construction workers, and their spouses, daughters, and sons. They energetically joined me in projecting the vision and providing sweat equity to rebuild the walls of Jerusalem. And we accomplished the task in just fifty-two days! Unfortunately spears, shields, and bows were as much a part of this construction project as doors, bolts, and bars, but we worked together repairing the spirits of the people of Judah and their land. (And no fox climbing on it could break it down! [Neh. 4:3]. All along the gracious hand of God was upon every one of us.

Nehemiah obviously was a person of prayer, someone who related to God daily and consciously in most everything. At first glance, Nehemiah's passion for people in unfortunate circumstances and for the environment appears to instigate his call to lead this rebuilding project. But from all we know about the situation, Nehemiah was not seeking to do something else with his life. He was at the right place at the right time and was spiritually pliant enough not to hesitate in responding to a God-given inner yearning. Also persons close to Nehemiah supported him and his vision to rebuild the wall. God certainly knew Nehemiah's gift of unusual empathy, his care in appraising a situation, his willingness to carry his work through to conclusion, and his capacity to raise the morale of the Jewish people. Above all, God knew that Nehemiah always would stay connected to "the great and awesome God who keeps covenant and steadfast love with those who love" God (Neh. 1:5).

As we review his story today, we recognize Nehemiah's natural talent as a strategic planner. He was able to organize a large number of people around a common endeavor of great magnitude. Such natural talent is an expression of God's common grace. We know that God has given each living person some natural talents, whether the ability to build a wall, organize a group, or play the piano. These natural talents vary from person to person in both degree and kind. "We have gifts that differ according to the grace given to us: prophecy, in proportion to faith; ministry, in ministering; the teacher, in teaching; the exhorter, in exhortation; the giver, in generosity; the leader, in diligence; the compassionate, in cheerfulness" (Rom. 12:6-7). If we all had the same gift—teaching, for example—who would minister to those needing pastoral care? Who would creatively design or construct furniture or vehicles for transportation? Who would perceive the suffering of others and organize volunteers to make soup kitchens and clothes closets accessible to the public?

Identifying Natural Gifts and Spiritual Gifts

We invite selectors to look beyond obvious natural gifts, which are important, to *spiritual gifts* in potential church leaders. Individuals with highly developed spiritual gifts use them because they have a passion for bringing together the "Spirit" and the "us" in congregational life. They use their gifts intentionally, openly, and reverently for building up God's reign on earth. As selectors, look for persons who say sincerely and enthusiastically, in one way or another, "I rely on God's guidance every step of the way. God does more and more of the work." Seek out persons whose sense of self is firmly grounded in God, who are at peace with who they are, who increasingly trust their own intuition, who are not afraid to imagine, and who desire to develop not only their own inner resources but those of others. Parker Palmer's writings stress that leadership blossoms when a person leads out of a truly integrated self. Authentic spiritual leaders speak from the deepest recesses of their hearts because they're steeped in prayer and worship, scripture and theology, dialogue and silence, as well as wholesome human and environmental relationships.

An integrated, self-differentiated spiritual leader possesses the capacity to see beyond the immediate time and place and engages a congregation in articulating what is seen with spiritual eyes. Is it perhaps this capacity that renders leadership possible, even rewarding, in times of peril as well as promise? How life-changing would it be for your congregation if selectors focused on potential leaders who are not only aware of their natural gifts but whose principal occupation is being holy?

Candidates and selectors need only to look to the charism of their denomination for inspiration about holiness. For example, Methodist and Wesleyan traditions call their members to move toward holiness by seeking the mind of Christ in their devotional lives as well as in their work for justice. They practice Christian conferencing. Members of Anabaptist, Brethren, and Mennonite traditions ask, "What would Jesus do?" Friends (Quakers) rely on God's Spirit speaking to individuals and the community through silence and inner light. How does your denomination challenge you to be holy?

Do selectors need to consider such spiritual gifts as the ability to embrace risk, immersion in the mission of the congregation, ability to befriend chaos and work in the midst of confusion? We think so. Other qualities worth seeking include: empathy with the poor and lonely, capacity to connect with diverse cultures in a congregation, living out of a worldview founded on dignity and justice for all, willingness to explore areas where "change" in simple procedures or in weighty church polity matters could invite the congregation into new discoveries about itself.

from Lydia, a Selectee

(based on Acts 16:14-15, 40)

It's true that I live a comfortable life in Thyatira as a businesswoman. I enjoy my profession as a dealer in rich purple cloth. Quite awhile ago I was baptized by Paul in the river. And, as my story goes, this blessing began to focus my purpose in life: to be a lover of God. That's my real calling.

Let me share with you a significant happening in my life. My soul was especially stirred by God one Sabbath morning as I joined a group of women gathered for prayer by the river. (This Sabbath prayer time had nourished our group for many months.) That was when I first met Paul, who found us at the river. He was looking for a group with whom to pray that morning.

When Paul spoke in our group, I was taken with his prayer and also with his teachings. I felt certain that the Spirit of God, who has always been evident in our midst, led Paul to our little group that day.

For whatever reason, Paul seemed to take special notice of me. My comments and questions connected with him at a deep level, and he generously affirmed my insights. In a sense, he was acknowledging what he probably didn't know: I was the one who facilitated the group's worship each Sabbath morning. Or perhaps he had intuited my leadership abilities.

That morning we learned how Paul traveled as a missionary preaching the good news of Jesus. Since he had such a warm, outgoing personality it appeared to us that he would be equally at home with Jews and Gentiles. We also discovered that he would be coming back to our town occasionally. So I invited him to stay with me when he returned. It took some convincing, but I finally persuaded him to accept my hospitality. As it turned out, we had great conversations about Jesus, about Paul's efforts to lure people into new spiritual insights and practices, about my growing awareness of the leadership abilities with which God has gifted me, and much more.

Between Paul's visits I continued to lead our little "house church" in Sabbath worship. This ritual has become essential for the nurture of our souls. And my leadership of this small group has become ever more centered in the desire to facilitate the connections among God's Spirit, the dynamics of our individual lives, and the life of our group. We attempt to plumb the depth of our lives in God by sharing joys and concerns, lifting them to God, and vowing to pray for one another during the week ahead.

Believe me, I'm sure of this: God places people in our lives who truly make a difference. Now I don't see Paul that often, but we both continue to proclaim the life and death of Jesus in our own ways—with gifts differing.

Using Personality and Spiritual Typology Instruments

A number of personality preference and spiritual typology instruments/resources are available to persons considering career changes or seeking more self-knowledge. Some of the information gleaned from such instruments may be helpful to selectors of church leaders. For the purpose of this book, we wish to lift up a few of the resources but not reiterate content available elsewhere. See the Resources section for publication information. Do some research on any resource in order to determine how to capitalize on its strengths. And understand the limitations of a resource in a particular selection circumstance. Perhaps an outside resource is not even necessary in your situation.

In *Discover Your Spiritual Type,* author Corinne Ware offers a framework for naming and understanding spiritual experience. She explains four spiritual types according to how one experiences God: intellectually, emotionally, mystically, or abstractly. Her book provides exercises and tools for individual and congregational use. Celia Hahn used this model in a project on congregational spirituality. Her book *Uncovering Your Church's Hidden Spirit* reports the results of that endeavor, which involved a number of church groups.

Isabel Briggs Myers developed the Myers-Briggs Type Indicator Personality Inventory, an instrument that distinguishes among sixteen personality types. It is used widely in both churches and industry in the United States. Candidates in a selection process who have taken this Indicator may share their "Type" with the selectors along with what they learned about themselves in the course of answering the Indicator's questions.

The Enneagram personality typology is not originally Christian but derived from the Eastern tradition of Sufi wisdom. One can use the Enneagram to discover one's personal spiritual typology in the midst of the spiritual journey. At a time when people are pondering how spiritual currents from the East and West meet, many authors are writing about the Enneagram. *Discovering the Enneagram: An Ancient Tool, a New Spiritual Journey* by Richard Rohr and Andreas Ebert is one basic resource among a number of titles.

Arthur F. Miller Jr. and William Hendricks describe a process called MAP (Motivated Abilities Pattern)—an insightful tool for self-understanding—in *Why You Can't Be Whatever You Want to Be.* The book discusses the intersection of abilities and motivating forces, part of each person's unique design.

Some ministry formation programs ask what are characterized as left- and right-brain questions of those discerning a call to ordained ministry. The Episcopal diocese of Nebraska's Plan for Ministry Development has adapted questions from *Listening Hearts: Discerning Call in Community* by Suzanne G. Farnham, Joseph P. Gill, R. Taylor McLean, and Susan M. Ward. For instance, a right-brain question asked of those pursuing a call to ordained ministry is this: "What image, color, or piece of music seems to represent your sense of call?"

The United Methodist Church of the Resurrection in Leawood, Kansas (13720 Roe Avenue, 913-897-0120, www.cor.org.), has published *Spiritual Gifts Discovery,* a fifty-four-page spiral handbook for congregational and personal use. Discovery exercises and worksheets are included.

The Roman Catholic Diocese of Kansas City–St. Joseph, Missouri, offers a three-year formation program for laity and clergy called New Wine. During the program of courses, those who seek to become leaders obtain a foundation in theology and pastoral skills. Two of the twelve courses are "Ministry and the Minister" and "Leadership." Among the goals of these courses are discovering one's gifts, understanding ministry as a response to God's call to live out one's faith in Jesus publicly and actively, and examining and developing leadership styles consistent with Christian values.

A book by C. Peter Wagner, *Your Spiritual Gifts Can Help Your Church Grow,* comments on twenty-seven spiritual gifts and the difference between gifts, talents, and roles.

Please Understand Me: Character and Temperament Types, by David Keirsey and Marilyn Bates, provides a useful vocabulary and phraseology for applying the Carl Jung–Isabel Myers concepts of personality type. The book contains a questionnaire and also a chapter on "Temperament in Leading."

Considering Spiritual Formation Disciplines

Candidates in a selection process may have experience or be participating in practices of spiritual formation that are pertinent to their spiritual discernment. Selectors need to be aware of such activities and explore the learnings of the candidates. Perhaps a candidate has experienced the Spiritual Exercises of Saint Ignatius during an eight-day or thirty-day retreat. The Spiritual Exercises are a means toward freeing the individual of all disordered attachments and finding God's yearning for the person's life.

A candidate may be receiving spiritual direction with a certified spiritual director, pursuing a deeper awareness of God's presence in every aspect of life. A directee attempts to grow in discerning love before God by naming and facing matters of self-delusion, unwillingness, or seeming inabilities that hinder spiritual life. A directee also seeks to grow in awareness of her or his spiritual gifts, which are given for building up the reign of God.

Perhaps the candidate regularly spends time at a retreat house or a hermitage, praying with scripture, reading other spiritual literature, exploring the beauties of nature, or journaling in an effort to gain self-knowledge. Invite candidates to talk about their spiritual gifts in the context of their spiritual life—how they are living it— and make some connections between their life and their understanding of spiritual leadership. Referring to Nehemiah's story, a framework for your conversation could be as follows:

- A call to ministry is initiated by God, though many people may be involved in its instigation, its expression.
- An authentic call is not vigorously sought by the individual being called.

- Elements of mystery accompany the call.
- God's timing of the call is significant and usually means more than first meets the eye.
- A call may be motivated by pain or a vision that things can be different.
- One's feelings do not determine the validity of the call. (The call is ultimately validated by the community for whom the call is activated.)

Selecting church leaders without reference to spiritual qualifications, that is, judging solely the ability to take care of temporal affairs of a church, usually results in less-than-spiritual leadership. Why don't we intentionally raise church leadership selection processes to the next level, a level at which spiritual gifts enhance and stimulate natural gifts?

The Church of the Brethren made a sweeping attempt to accomplish such a shift at its Conference 2000. The denomination passed a resolution on congregational structure that updated and improved its 1992 *Manual of Organization and Polity*. The new model asks each congregation to shape its life around mission (what it is called to be) and vision (what it is called to do) and to discern spiritual gifts. The new congregational model includes a Gifts Discernment Team made up of the pastor or a member of the pastoral team, a moderator, a deacon, and one woman and one man from the congregation at large.

Among the responsibilities of the Gifts Discernment Team are these: (1) to educate the congregation on discernment of spiritual gifts, (2) to receive the names of members under consideration for specific ministries during a special time of prayer during a congregational forum, (3) to oversee talent/interest/skill inventories, and (4) to serve as a contact team for district and denominational groups responsible for calling leaders. The congregational forum (the church in business session), which meets following a Sunday morning worship service, affirms or confirms each person's call to a particular ministry. This change in congregational structure, while nurturing the Church of the Brethren membership, may give witness to the broader church as well.

A BIBLICAL WITNESS
The Voice of the Twelve
(based on Matthew 10)

Our first reaction is amazement. Jesus has called us to be his special and close followers, teaching and leading the people of our cities and towns as he is teaching and leading them. We are such a motley group! We have different skills and trades and worldly interests. Some of us understand less than others what Jesus is asking of us.

What does Jesus see in us that inspired him to call us as his apostles? (By the way, the word *apostle* is really not a title, honorary or otherwise. The word simply means "one who is sent.") We think Jesus has been keeping his eyes open for people who have a deep personal relationship with God, who have a sense of urgency about Jesus' mission. We assume that he has spent a great deal of prayer time discerning who could be proclaimers of the good news. We know that we hold his deepest values. And as different as we apostles are, we have been impressed by the common power his words and actions have on us.

Undoubtedly Jesus is aware of how far we are from being accomplished leaders, and we know we still have a lot more to learn from him. Shortly after he called us, Jesus gave us serious instruction on how to collaborate with him in his work. Because he feels that the people in the cities and villages are "like sheep without a shepherd" (Matt. 9:36), he told us that we are called to proclaim loudly, wisely, and widely all that he has taught us. In other words, we are to teach, witness, distribute food to the hungry, and offer signs and wonders in his name.

We still need to develop skills. And we all wonder about the deep suffering he tells us will be part of our shared story. But we all assent to giving this call our best effort. For now we are taking to heart all Jesus' instructions: humbly serving the people with passion and compassion as he serves them, calling forth the best in them; continuing to learn to see as Jesus sees, with spiritual eyes; and remaining faithful to prayer, the heart of our shared calling.

❖

6

CONSIDERING
INCLUSIVITY

In this chapter we will not offer a final word about selecting church leaders via the lens of inclusion and exclusion, but we do intend to suggest matters for consideration by selectors and means of approaching the issues through dialogue. It is our experience that significant issues surrounding age, gender, lay and clergy, race and ethnicity, sexual orientation, and quotas related to any of these categories often surface in selection processes, whether in local congregations, judicatory/diocesan settings, or in the selection of denominational leaders. In turn, those selected as church leaders will face those same significant inclusivity issues during their time of service. So we will look at some serious and potentially divisive matters currently facing church leaders, matters that the church would like to bring to closure soon.

The Difficult Nature of Inclusivity Issues

Whether issues of inclusion and exclusion stem from the doctrinal life of the church, are liturgical in nature, or call into question long-held moral standards, they are vast and complex. They not only provoke academic disagreements but often tear at relationships among the body of Christ. Some matters involving the role of conscience leave a little room for respectful dissent within denominational life; others prompt the church to act like the Hatfields and McCoys. Some issues are so complex that they divert attention from mission, drain energy, fuel anxiety, and paralyze meetings.

Every faith community has the right to establish clear standards for its leadership. Educational requirements, mental and emotional stability, gifts and graces, understanding of theology, polity, and governance are obvious touchstones in the selection process. The community's unique history, tradition, and character may fine-tune the standards. Community members therefore have the right to exclude. But at the same time every faith community has the duty to consider prayerfully the full range of giftedness that lies within its membership. The Spirit may nudge the community to reconsider persons who may have been kept on the edge. So with the right to exclude comes the duty to consider inclusion.

In one pioneer missionary effort in Africa, a man whose family included two wives was converted to Christianity. That conversion set the nascent Christian community into a discernment mode: to include or to exclude? After prayer and consultation they decided to include the man and his wives in full membership, but they would exclude them from any eventual consideration as elders. The church had the right to exclude and the duty to consider to include.

Inclusivity issues often sprout advocacy groups. Slavery was such an issue in the past. Racism has been another. We have no way of knowing which issues will be divisive in the future (perhaps biogenetics will become divisive for church bodies), but we choose to touch on a few of them in the contemporary church, in hopes that the practice of spiritual discernment might offer a more prayerful and reflective way to be church together at this time.

The reality of constantly advancing technology has brought people of every place and status to growing awareness that human beings are incredibly diverse in social customs and views of the world. The Internet connects people of every culture, religion, and social stratum at any hour of the day or night. At this time in history we also know that not everyone in the church believes in an unchangeable hierarchy or organizational scheme of status and roles, regardless of denomination or length of the church's existence. Not everyone in the world believes that church documents, decrees, and policies are without intrinsic contradictions. And there seems no way to call off a contemporary deluge of new and challenging information in virtually every discipline—whether the social sciences, theology, or technology. The church, a living system, probably will continue to be hard-pressed to respond and develop within the natural environment that challenges it without losing its integrity or identity.

A story told about Albert Einstein relates that he handed out a final exam to his physics students, and one complained, "These are the very same questions you gave us on last year's exam!" "Yes, I know they are the same," Einstein replied. "But the answers have changed." That remark pretty much sums up the state of the church in the world today: We are in the midst of struggling to be church as we've known "church," but a number of questions just won't go away, and some of the old answers don't seem to fit neatly anymore.

Margaret Wheatley writes that "self-reference is what facilitates orderly change in turbulent environments."[1] She surely is not writing about a closed system that "walls out" and "walls in" serious questions or answers but a system in which resources and relationships properly used and maintained constantly facilitate the core identity of a group. How do we as church allow our resources and relationships to facilitate our identity in the midst of a changing world and the societal issues that cause varying degrees of turmoil among us? Congregations and denominations can expect diversity of opinions and approaches, but commitment to ongoing dialogue, to pastoral care of one another—especially when matters under consideration have red flags—may help us to live toward the ideal Paul described to the people of Corinth. Remember the setting: A better educated minority was behind Apollos, a Jewish convert from Alexandria; another group boasted of their attachment to the apostle Peter; a third group, the majority, followed Paul; and a fourth group prided itself on a singular relationship with Christ. Paul admonished the quarreling community: "Now I appeal to you, brothers and sisters, by the name of our Lord Jesus Christ, that all of you be in agreement and that there be no divisions among you, but that you be united in the same mind and the same purpose" (1 Cor. 1:10). That's the ideal. Our contemporary church still has a long way to go to reach it!

Approaching Inclusion/Exclusion Issues as Selectors

We offer here some basic questions for selectors to consider not only in choosing leaders but in future conversation about the life of the congregation as it evolves. The answers will be unique to your congregation and situation. Your answers may come from insights gained by telling your congregation's story, then reflecting on it biblically and theologically.

- What does your denomination require regarding quotas, balance, representations, and so forth, for local church leadership councils, teams, staffs, and so forth?
- How much leeway exists for local adaptation?

- How long have local policies been in place; have they ever been changed?
- Have policy changes brought newer forms of provincialism?
- How well do current policies serve emerging needs?
- How well do policies reinforce your congregation's vision?
- How might future visions involve departures (major or minor) from your present policies?
- Do you need to petition to alter any denominational specifications that hinder rather than support your work?
- What in your policies is purely incidental?
- What in your selection policies is indispensable to the community. Why?
- What aspects of your selection policies encourage community building and promote conversation among selectors?
- What elements in your policies proceed from a sense of being on a journey of conversion (not necessarily radical conversion) and promote a sense of being in a graced process of renewal?
- Which policies address dissension among members?
- What adjectives describe the character of your denominational policies, such as, strong, harsh, reasonable?

The leadership bodies of many local congregations often spend hours exploring how to raise money, how to care for aging buildings, arguing about the style or content of worship services or the number of paid staff, or trying to figure out how to improve programs or attendance at programs. Some of that energy is undoubtedly necessary and worthwhile. At the same time, the leadership of some local congregations give short shrift to matters of inclusivity. They may prefer to think that the issues will go away, or they may be oblivious to the need for creative and realistic thinking and planning.

While some churches really *live* in their neighborhoods, others don't see the changing scene around them.

When the church ignores, unconsciously screens out, or excludes people from church leadership or membership because of race or gender or puts individuals out to pasture because of age, the church is not able to learn from the human and spiritual gifts these persons offer. Nor can the church attend to the needs of those who are not fully in our midst. Though it is virtually impossible for anyone to walk in another person's shoes, we can learn to walk respectfully together along the same path.

The New Testament presents an image of the church as a community created by the Holy Spirit that seeks to live as an alternative, inclusive culture. Its identity—"where two or three are gathered in my name, I am there among them" (Matt. 18:20)—is rooted in biblical story: "Now that faith has come, we are no longer subject to a disciplinarian, for in Christ Jesus you are all children of God through faith. As many of you as were baptized into Christ have clothed yourselves with Christ. There is no longer Jew or Greek, there is no longer slave or free, there is no longer male and female; for all of you are one in Christ Jesus. And if you belong to Christ, then you are Abraham's offspring, heirs according to the promise" (Gal. 3:25-29). Though some interpreters suggest that this passage endorses an end to sexism and discrimination of every kind, others today regard this interpretation as a bit naive. Yet isn't it exciting to think about this text's being prophetic beyond the vision of the author?

Consider your own church community. Among selectors—as well as within the congregation as a whole—can people express divergent theological views and opinions while maintaining a climate of sincere respect for one another—that self-reference which "facilitates orderly change in turbulent environments"? Or is there a need to move beyond the security, isolation, and dependence on past ways of operating and invisible structures that haven't been verbalized in order to create and sustain that climate of respect? Some selection committees have an unspoken agreement not to talk about anything that could cause dissension, that is, until the last minute when people become impatient and frustrated about what is being said or not said; this behavior leads to heated arguments in the end.

If the selection climate needs change or the selection policies need improvement, take the time to do your collegial homework. Mary Benet McKinney, in her apt description of spiritual discernment, speaks about a time for "turning up the heat." She means taking time for intense, prayerful consideration of every option and its ramifications—not putting on boxing gloves for conversation!

The thesis of Joseph Campbell's book *The Hero with a Thousand Faces* is that there is really only one story and one hero, and the hero wears many faces, including our own. Campbell says that the hero of a story always journeys with two inseparable companions: conflict and new beginnings. This is the story of the church, which is to say that every one of our churches meets some obstacles on its journey; we're constantly in need of mending relationships and starting over. Whether you are working on a small- or grand-scale selection process, we invite you to be in loving dialogue, in prayerful consideration, and to give your best efforts toward overcoming differences, remaining always connected to the "Spirit" and the "us" in the process.

If the following witness were given in today's church, the elder could (in many denominations) be male or female. What message (clear or subtle) do you hear about the importance of being inclusive from the following story?

from an Elder of Israel, a Selectee
(based on Exodus 18)

I was one of those who rejoiced over the narrow escape from the Egyptians as we fled their land. But, yes, I also was one of the complainers during those long days in the wilderness under the leadership of Moses. At times life back in Egypt looked better than what we were experiencing.

During that time when we were trying to find our way in a new life under new leadership, something happened that changed my life and outlook. Jethro, Moses' father-in-law, came for a visit, bringing Moses' wife, Zipporah, and their two sons. We loved Jethro at first sight. He was one of those desert priests who seemed to have so much wisdom. Desert spirituality must have been cultivated for centuries! He wanted to hear our story, and Moses gave him a blow-by-blow account. Jethro summed it all up when he named how God had been present to us, surely a God more powerful than all the gods of Egypt. He connected this God with the one who had been the subject of much discussion and reflection by the campfire in former days—the God revealed in the burning bush at this very mountain.

Jethro stayed around for a few days, observing Moses' performance as a leader. He offered some free consultation: "This is not good. You are trying to do it all by yourself. People are waiting in line for you all day. You will wear yourself out and all these people with you." He suggested an alternative paradigm for leadership: (1) Represent the people before God—not the other way around by representing God to the people; (2) teach and instruct the people so they can make choices based on firm values and statutes; (3) choose other responsible persons who can share leadership with you and build in an accountability measure—by thousands, hundreds, fifties, and tens.

Jethro also laid out some common baseline qualifications for individuals in leadership: (1) Whoever is chosen should be "able . . . among all the people." In other words, they should have skills that have been proven in the community; (2) Whoever is chosen should fear God; (3) Whoever is chosen should be trustworthy, possessing a strong inner aversion to dishonest gain—especially in leadership.

Somehow, with those qualifications, my name surfaced toward the top of the list, and I was selected. I never would have sought this position on my own. But that careful process, facilitated by Jethro, a spiritual giant whom I trusted, gave me the courage to say yes to the call and the confidence to go ahead.

❖

Specific Issues Facing the Church

For the last several years Worshipful-Work has been introducing a process of spiritual discernment into decision making at all levels of the ecumenical church. In so doing, we have been drawn into difficult arenas. Every denomination is in the midst of decisions related to (1) the welcome of homosexuals into its membership; (2) the blessing of same-sex marriages; and (3) the inclusion of gay and lesbian persons as clergy or lay leaders; or all three.

That struggle is the source of ever-threatening division among local churches and denominations. With an increasing number of resolutions to vote "for" or "against," more and more persons are finding themselves in the middle struggling with the issue. One presbytery, which took a day to consider the ordination question, assumed the members were split down the middle on the issue. At the end of the day, the facilitator asked each small group to select one person from the group to speak his or her own passion—not the group's report—back to the plenary session. To the surprise of many, instead of selecting strong proponents of one side or the other, the groups selected persons who were struggling in the middle.

Our use of legislative process within a parliamentary culture may have served the church well selectively in the past, but that same process is not currently serving us well. It makes for winners and losers and does not allow enough space and time to be in the middle. People need to come to rest—either in one mind or in one spirit—ideally in both.

Historians are now noting how long the church has taken to make some important decisions. They point to decades and even centuries of attitude change regarding the place of slavery and the role of women. Gay/lesbian issues too may be in for a long ride rather than a quick resolution.

Our current decision-making process is slanted toward closing on a decision—sometimes coming to a quick fix or making an efficient determination. Peter Senge, director of the Organizational Learning Center at Massachusetts Institute of Technology, points to the difference between *discussion* and *dialogue*. Discussion is an attempt to close on a deliberation—to prevail, as in a game of table tennis. Dialogue, on the other hand, holds the matter up in the air and allows the group to stay with it for a good length of time. We in church systems do not do well in dialogue, simmering toward a conclusion. We know how to turn up the legislative heat. And that is where we are now.

A number of divided church bodies have declared multiyear moratoriums on resolutions in order to provide an opportunity for the church to continue study and reflection on the matter. The Reformed Church in America has given itself a sabbatical from political debate on policy issues related to homosexuality because these matters already have been thoroughly addressed by previous synods. Now Reformed Church leaders want to enable congregations and the classis that governs them to enter a process of intentional spiritual discernment concerning the pastoral challenges over a two-year period.

Because we often don't know how to sit with one another, in-depth study and dialogue rarely happen. Opposing advocacy and resistance groups regard an extension of time as an opportunity to collect money, rearm, and plot strategies for the next round of debate. A matter kept up in the air turns into a costly legislative process, hardly a dialogue. An ongoing ritual of fights depletes the church's energy and resources.

Another denomination, the Disciples of Christ, recently has agreed not to vote immediately on two issues: their understanding of biblical interpretation, and the challenge of racism. Instead, each issue is being submitted to a six-year spiritual discernment process for reflection, discussion, prayer, and sharing throughout the church. Following that time, the denomination will look at the perspectives and directions that have emerged churchwide.

Many people in the postmodern context agree that dealing with weighty denominational issues by fiat is not helpful. The hierarchy of the Roman Catholic Church has for many years declared that women are unsuited for the priesthood, saying and writing again and again that women are "different but equal." These words tell many women that they lack the equality that would enable them to share in the governance, decision making, and sacramental life of the church. Yet, on the other hand, some women, while very educated and very sensitive to issues of mutuality in the church, believe that the admission of women into the present clerical structure of the Roman Catholic Church would exacerbate the contradictions in today's church. Many women and men (lay and ordained) say that differences in worldview, theological and scriptural insight, and practical opinion on this matter are not just a peripheral view. Instead this view reflects the struggle of a church made up of limited, fallible women and men "to become the sacrament of the full personhood of all people in the grace of Christ."[2] Women in traditions that limit participation in ministry because of gender are not looking for signs that they might eventually be useful because of the shortage of men but signs that the ministries women perform are genuinely needed in the church. This would mean an admission that the church has been wrong in the past.

Ordination of women is a live issue in conservative Protestant denominations as well. The media highlighted it during the summer of 2000 when the Southern Baptist Convention prohibited the ordination of women. No doubt this prohibition presents a serious situation for women preparing for ordained ministry, but perhaps the problem is more serious for women already ordained in this denomination. Their ordinations may be accepted by the memberships of some local congregations, but when it comes to "call" and "placement," the playing field of ordained ministry surely will be significantly narrowed.

This many-faceted issue hasn't gone away and probably will not disappear in this decade. Theological conversation about women's ordination will continue in a variety of arenas. Spiritual vision, the demands of the gospel, and a good dose of individual and collective humor about the issue seem to enable many women to stay in the church today. Women have taken upon themselves the task of finding liberating and empowering situations in otherwise patriarchal traditions. Despite their frustrations with the institutional church, women say they need to remain within the structure in order to help change it.

Perspectives on Struggling with Issues

We offer the voices of three important figures, teachers from the disciplines of spiritual discernment and dialogue out of the past and in current times: John Cassian, a fourth-century church father of the desert; Ignatius Loyola, a sixteenth-century founder/leader of a religious order, the Jesuits; and Peter Senge, a contemporary voice in organizational and leadership science (see Resources). What can we hear in their commentary that might help in the struggles of today's church?

John Cassian, Egyptian abba of the desert, wrote about the process of spiritual discernment in *The Conferences*. He poses soul-searching questions for anyone who would adopt the practice of spiritual discernment. Ignatius Loyola introduced imagination and the role of feelings—consolation and desolation—into a rationally oriented culture of decision making and guidance. The Jesuits place discernment in the midst of the faith community, where spiritual formation is taking place.

In *The Fifth Discipline* Peter Senge advocates learning communities in which genuine discussion and dialogue can take place. Senge includes mutual respect for one another as one of three conditions for dialogue— along with the creation of a safe context in which a facilitator keeps the dialogue moving. Just getting together will not do it. Another author, Ronald A. Heifitz, echoes this theme in *Leadership without Easy Answers* when he calls for a "holding environment" in which groups can make their adaptive changes. While trying to introduce a patient and prayerful process into the church's decision-making procedures, we can turn to these and other voices to draw some threads that might be woven together into a useful contemporary process.

LETTING GO OF INVESTMENT, ATTACHMENT, AND OUTCOME

Dietrich Bonhoeffer says that we all come to community with a "wish dream," that is, a picture of how this community will be shaped and will function. He suggests that the best thing Jesus can do is disillusion us about our wish dreams until we realize that Christ himself is the only basis of our life together.[3] Asking "not my will but thy will" has never been easy. Jesus sweat blood in his response. John Cassian asks, Is this potential path "heavy with the fear of God?"[4]

Cassian asks another important question: Is a decision genuine in the feelings that underlie it? Anything short of serious grappling with an issue will not do. Ignatius Loyola offers the concept of "coming to indifference," that is, indifference to anything but seeking and doing the will of God. We tend to regard indifference as a negative, I-don't-care attitude. The Jesuits call for indifference as a foundation for spiritual discernment.

The stakes seem so high for both sides in the gay and lesbian issue that indifference seems impossible—like a betrayal of principle and a loss of self. But self-differentiation needs to go deeper than the causes to which one is attached. Only relinquishment can test the degrees to which a person's attachments and investments are subconsciously or overtly conditioned by tradition or contemporary culture.

Peter Senge's other condition for genuine dialogue is willingness to "suspend assumptions." That does not necessarily mean that we surrender assumptions but that we hold them up for the community to see and then sit loosely with them, open to hearing other voices.

One sure sign that relinquishment is taking place would be the dissolution of advocacy and resistance groups on both sides. If such groups divested themselves of treasuries and mailing lists and returned conversation and energy to the forums of church bodies, we might be able to sit with one another in a new way. Another of John Cassian's questions is, Has vainglory lessened the discernment's merit? We often plaster our individual and collective egos all over our deliberations.

Theological disciplines call for hearing one another's stories, placing these stories in dialogue with the tradition, then surfacing meanings, values, and beliefs. From that foundation we can create preferred visions of the future and discern God's yearning in the current contexts. Scripture plays a prominent role in that process. Organizational development theorists like Peter Senge also operate from a value-based premise. The role of a board, for instance, is to focus on mission-based values and to develop the organization accordingly.

A process of spiritual discernment requires identifying guiding principles. Sometimes in the church we operate as if we are of one mind. As to whether gay and lesbian persons should be selected as church leaders, one camp adopts justice as its guiding principle; the other camp adopts biblical morality. The two camps can and will debate the issue without an open exploration of the guiding principles that underlie their positions.

Spiritual discernment calls the participants to sit with one another long enough to probe their own and one another's guiding principles. A patient examination may surface contradictions and shadows that were not apparent earlier. Might the stories in the fullness of scripture contain gaps or contradictions? Might the love and justice sides of Jesus interact with strange twists? Ignatius invites the discerner to *improve* the position opposite one's own, giving it the best attributes as a way of testing to discover hidden qualities.

CONSOLATION OR DESOLATION?

The Jesuits introduced feelings into spiritual discernment, asking whether a potential course of action would leave one at ease or uneasy. But the Jesuits go deeper. *Consolation* also leaves one closer to God, whereas in *desolation* one has the impression of distance from God's presence. Even after a tentative decision has been made, the Jesuits ask us to place the matter on our hearts to see how the decision rests. That testing and resting may take a good long time. In that resting Cassian speaks again: Is a course of action "too light because of human ostentation or some novel presumption"?[5] Only time will tell about passing fads and incomplete information. Do we really have enough information and wisdom to decide finally?

Current discussions in World Council of Churches circles (with input from the Greek Orthodox Church) and in Anglican circles offer another word for our consideration: *acceptance*. The Greek Orthodox Church points out that while thirteen councils claimed to speak authoritatively in the early history of the church, eventually the church recognized only six or seven of them as authoritative. What made the difference? Acceptance! The final step in a decision is whether or not and how the decision is recognized as being of the Spirit of God. Has it been implemented into the life of the church? Answering that question takes years, maybe centuries. Perhaps the best final test will be to see how a choice is working or not working out over a long period of time. Even then, the dialogue will need to continue.

FOR HOW LONG?

In describing the contrast between discussion and dialogue, Peter Senge suggests that learning communities will develop a rhythm between the two—knowing how long to hold a matter up in the air and when to close it down in a final decision. (The timing question even calls us into spiritual discernment!) This is tough for the church: "How long?" "How long must folks wait?" "How long must we put up with this discussion?" We may just have to wait for God's Spirit, who will lead us into all truth. What if the Spirit said, "Well, what do you know about that! Church, let's sit down together and figure this one out."

In the meantime we could listen to what Peter Senge is saying about the nature of organizational change in his book *The Dance of Change*. There are two ways to view institutions, he says— either as machines or as organisms. If we emphasize the church as a machine, we will look for leaders who can be mechanics and fix the machine, one way or another. Rules, procedures, and the importance of the ordained (clergy or lay) will dominate. On the other hand, if we look at the church as an organism, we will look for gardeners in leadership roles. Senge observes that after ten years of trying to transform organizations, he's come to the conclusion that we cannot change institutions from the top down. Instead we should look for teams of people at any level in the organization who are doing meaningful work and who have a sense of joy about it. If this joy is authentic, we can trust that they will be seed carriers, spreading their influence throughout the system, thereby changing it.

While we are simmering toward decisions in weighty matters for the church, let us not count God short. What if God said, "While the church is simmering in the soup pot, short of a final decision, I think I will unleash a cadre of storytellers, sages, teachers, servants, and compassionate caregivers!" God's presence would free us from some of our institutional and mechanistic ways. God's presence just might release organic ministries that would serve God's purpose, bringing blessings to the church.

Given the sensitive nature of stressful selection issues facing the church today, how shall we proceed? We again affirm the right and need to set standards that may lead to exclusion—but at the same time affirm the duty under the Spirit of God to consider inclusion of gifted and called persons. Within this right and obligation, we pray for the Spirit of God to grace the selection participants and process. The tension calls for prayerful, sensitive, and open discernment. There is no other way.

We have here not the final word on the dilemma of inclusion and exclusion in selecting church leaders. But we have attempted to broach this topic and offer some question to help selectors delve into real issues in congregational life. We hope our thoughts shed new light on metaphors, narratives, and images that shape your individual perspectives and communal views. Within the echoes of the voices of Peter Senge, Ignatius Loyola, and John Cassian, let us covenant to sit together until we come to rest in one spirit or one mind. Anything else will divide the church, compromise its witness, and waste its resources.

7

SPIRITUAL DISCERNMENT
FOR SELECTEES

Thus far we have focused attention primarily on the discernment process of selectors. This coin has a flip side that is equally important. Selectees face a big decision—to say yes or to say no. It takes two to tango. Even if the answer is no, nothing is wasted in the economy of God's grace. God will use the interactive dancing between the selectors and the selectees as a means to bring clarity to both.

You may be the one in a quandary about how to process an invitation to a leadership role. The struggle may be an agonizing one, full of doubt as well as excitement and a sense of opportunity. You do not want to jump in too soon without carefully weighing the matter. Discernment comes knocking at the door of your heart or gut or mind: What to do? When to do? How to do? Or if to do?

The Lonely Path

How do you respond when the invitation to serve comes out of the blue with no advance hint or warning? At times nominating and selecting groups or individuals engage in a private process, come to a conclusion, and then extend an offer or invitation. Your name may have come to a group's attention without your awareness. You may not have imagined the particular calling as one you would ever consider. Perhaps the role is so unthinkable or distasteful that the immediate response is to reject it.

To complicate matters, the nature of the process or the role may be so confidential that you are limited to seeking wisdom from a small circle of advisers. The path to decision is a lonely one, sometimes intensified by a narrow window of opportunity in which to reach the final answer. Time for a patient and prayerful discernment process seems alarmingly short. The pressure is on. How are you to proceed?

1. *Get in touch with your own story and the story of the inviting organization/faith group.* Look back over your life journey, naming the important forks in the road and the decisions you have made at those junctures. Allow your story line to break naturally into phases or stages. Label the stages. Ask yourself, "Who were the wise people who influenced me in each of those stages?" Look for signs of God's presence and the ministry of God's Spirit within the story. What accomplishments (in your own eyes) leave you feeling satisfied or even proud? What special gifts and abilities did you use in the pursuit of each accomplishment? What patterns may be projected into this new venture? With what biblical story, theme, or character do aspects of your story connect? Does your story express a destiny or life purpose that you need to bring to fruition? Perhaps you feel you were born to do _____ or really be _____. Fill in the blanks.

2. *Deal honestly with the flattery.* When surprised with an invitation to take a position in the church, many folks immediately sense it as an honor and affirmation. That feeling may feed their ego a bit and puff them up to a degree that makes deep, honest self-examination difficult. Vanity clouds the atmosphere of discernment. The fathers of the desert repeatedly warned their fellow monks about the dangers of

human show or vanity. They always linked discernment with humility, suggesting that humility is a prerequisite to discernment. Self-examination is the key. Ask yourself, "Would I try to prove something about myself to others in this role? Would this role make me a 'somebody' in contrast to my present feeling of being a 'nobody'?" Draw Jesus into the center of this examination, recalling John the Baptist's attitude, "I am not worthy to carry his sandals" (Matt. 3:11). Placing God at the center can clear the clouds that flattery may have created.

3. *Face the doubts.* You may doubt that you are worthy or that you know enough or that you are spiritual enough to take on the role offered to you. You may hold stereotypes about what church leaders look like and can't envision yourself in that picture. You may not have imagined that you could be a leader. You may carry unresolved inner conflicts or the burden of unresolved sin, which hold you back. Whether on your own or with the counsel of a pastor or friend, begin by naming the doubts and fears that could block your saying yes. Next release them to God. Being honest about your doubts and fears can release you from their power. Ongoing counsel will provide a more realistic appraisal of the significance of the doubts.

4. *Unscramble your priorities.* You unwittingly may have created a rut for yourself. An invitation to a new role may elicit a quick "no" response because your routine is set; instead, approach an invitation to leadership as a great opportunity to evaluate how you are using time and energy. Ask, "Where do my current priorities lie if ranked by the amount of time, energy, passion, and money that I put into them? Based on my current values and faith commitments, do I want to maintain this ranking?" Facing the question of new responsibility provides a moment to consider one's calling in life—both in the secular world of ministry and service and in the life and witness of the faith group. Align your priorities.

5. *Gather information.* In addition to getting in touch with the story and charism of the organization, look at the organization's past leaders. How have they influenced the church's story? Examine the church's documents to learn the foundations upon which it bases its ministry.

We recall a rather suspicious and critical nominee to church office who read, for the first time, the ten or so opening pages of the *Book of Order* of the Presbyterian Church (U.S.A.). She was overwhelmed with the way those basic principles connected with her spirit and values. Those pages read like an inspiring religious tract to her! The experience triggered a conversion in her attitude about what the real church was about. Try reading your church's foundational publications, such as *The Book of Discipline of The United Methodist Church* or *Vatican Council II: The Conciliar and Post Conciliar Documents*. You will find such material far from dry reading! Ask to see the Articles of Incorporation and By-laws of your local church. Look at the organizational structure. Is it freeing and open? Or is it constraining and closed? Gather information and ask questions!

6. *Consult spiritual guides.* The Quaker practice of providing a Clearness Committee for persons making an important decision offers a helpful model. You may be part of an existing small group (preferably two to five persons with whom you hold mutual trust and confidentiality). You may choose to take these group members into your confidence. Their role is not so much to give advice as to ask timely and probing questions, which you may or may not choose to answer on the spot. You may mull over those questions in your own private time.

You may choose to construct a temporary small group or seek out those persons you trust, seeing them either together as a group or individually. You could seek out a spiritual director. A gifted and sensitive person could be a real gift. Guidance from a spiritual director can help you focus on the inner movements of the Spirit that prompt you to let go, to take hold, and to name God's presence.

7. *Be attentive to signs along the way—signals of God's presence or signs that suggest a course of action.* These signs may seem a bit eerie or even mystical, but don't dismiss them. One friend of ours kept seeing the name of a particular city pop up in so many circumstances that he had to pay attention to any ways that God might be leading or calling him to that city. Listen to your dreams. Write them down and see if any patterns begin to emerge. Take time to release the imagination and let it roam. Use guided imagery or biblical imagery in concert with the more rational deliberation processes.

A BIBLICAL WITNESS

from Gideon, a Selectee
(based on Judges 6–7)

When people hear my name, they usually recall the great battle I led to defeat our oppressors the Midianites. Those scoundrels had been destroying our crops and taking our animals for years. My people, the Israelites, cowered before them, hiding out in mountains and caves with fear and trembling. You may recall how we tricked them. Instead of gathering a large army, I selected only three hundred warriors—those who drank out of their hands at the stream with their heads raised in watchfulness. I gave a trumpet and a jar lamp to each warrior. Then we sneaked into the Midianites' camp, although we were enormously outnumbered. On signal we all blew our trumpets and uncovered the lit lamps. The sound and light triggered a reaction of confusion and fear. The Midianites turned on one another, and we prevailed in a tremendous victory. That is the end of the story, but I want you to know the beginning of the story, for an important personal decision actually moved Israel toward this happy conclusion.

As I said, our people had been fearful of this mighty and savage enemy. Israel had forgotten the great story of our deliverance from the hand of the Egyptians generations earlier. And the people had forgotten the instruction to honor Yahweh and not Baal, god of the neighboring people. But I remembered the words of a prophet who had told us that old story. After a while it got under my skin.

I remember well the day I was threshing wheat—not on the threshing floor, for that would have exposed our resources to the Midianites. No, I was fearfully hiding out in the winepress to thresh my wheat. Suddenly I felt the penetrating eyes of a stranger who was sitting in the shade of an oak tree watching me. He was not of my people and was not a Midianite. In retrospect, I realize he was an angel of the Lord. At least he spoke wisdom born of God. In fact, he offered me a blessing, saying, "The Lord is with you, you mighty warrior!" "Ridiculous," I shouted back, laughing into his face. "If I am blessed, then what am I doing hiding out in fear, and why is all this happening to my people? Where is this God of old who delivers a people?" (I was kind of rough on him!)

Following the blessing, the stranger offered a daunting commission: "Go in this might of yours [did he mean my spunkiness?] and deliver Israel from the hand of Midian." I protested, "You see how weak I am. You probably know that my family is not wealthy or prominent—not a leading family. And I am the younger and weaker of my brothers. Get lost."

But the man persisted. Gradually the message sank in and began to get a hold on me. I could not forget it or shake it. That message was always on my mind, as was Moses' call to deliver Israel from the grip of Pharaoh. So my next step was a bold one. I asked for a sign—not one but three in succession. Each one led to another as the stakes and risk increased.

The visitor initiated the first sign. He instructed me to prepare an offering of meat and cake, which I did. When he touched the rock where I had placed the offering, fire consumed the meat and cake. I tell you, it was enough to make a believer out of me! And it was as if I had been face-to-face with the presence of God! The blessing, which the visitor then bestowed on me, was equally reassuring: "Peace be to you; do not fear, you shall not die" (Judg. 6:23).

That assurance provided an inner boldness that followed and prompted me through the next course of events. The altar to Baal standing in my father's yard increasingly became an offense to me. So one night I hitched up a team of oxen and pulled it down. You can imagine the rage of all the neighbors, for they believed Baal would ensure the success of our crops! But to my surprise, my own father came to my defense, saying that if Baal was really all-powerful, Baal could defend himself. That insight became a second sign for me.

The third sign came after I had summoned all of the tribes together to defend Israel against the Midianites. Fear continued to dominate them. I put a fleece of wool out overnight two nights in a row, asking God for a sign of favor over our enemies. On a dewless dry night the fleece was wet, while on a dewy wet night, it was dry. I took that as a sign, and we proceeded.

You had better believe that I now watch for signs—little or big ones, ordinary or extraordinary ones. God uses them along with the ancient story of deliverance and the lively words of the prophets to alleviate our doubts and fears.

WITNESS FROM A SELECTEE
the fictitious Evangel Kirk

Our historic Old First Church was about to celebrate its 125th anniversary. I first heard about the anniversary in a passing reference at an annual congregational meeting nearly two years ago. I didn't pay much attention to that mention because the event seemed far off and of no immediate concern to me. But all that changed.

One evening the president of the church board called asking to visit with me about an important church matter. I could not imagine what that might be but was intrigued enough to agree to the appointment. Both he and our pastor showed up at the door, and when we were settled they sprang a huge surprise on me. They asked me to consider chairing the 125th anniversary celebration effort.

You can imagine my first reaction: "Why me?" I am too young to remember much about the church. I never was a history buff, although I like a good story. I was not raised in this church as were some other third- and fourth-generation members. I have small children at home. I have never before exercised an important leadership role that did not include family or children's activities. (In other words, I am an unproven entity!) In protest I offered a tentative no.

The president and pastor were persistent folks. They could see that beneath my protest was a certain fire and spunk. They must have liked those traits and believed in God's power to take little old me and make something work. They countered, "We will give you three weeks to pray about this and give it consideration. In the meantime we will pray for you and ask you to do something. Conduct private and informal conversational interviews with people in the church—those who have been around for a long time and other relative newcomers like yourself. Ask people why they came to this church and why they have stayed." That assignment was hard to resist; I like people and have a natural gift of conversation. I agreed.

During those next three weeks I was converted. As I listened to the stories and later entered them into a journal, I became caught up in their deep mystery and significance. I discovered important common themes. I discovered that the church was far more than a building and more than the extension of able and beloved pastors. I discovered that when the church seemed weak and vulnerable, divine graces strengthened it. God is alive here.

A dream began to form in my mind. The 125th anniversary celebration could be a celebration of stories. If everyone could be as moved and affected as I was by such stories, then it was a ministry worthy of my energy and gifts. One day before the three weeks were up, I called the church board president and said, "Yes. This will be a privilege and opportunity to embark on a spiritual journey with my new committee and with every member of the congregation—especially the families and children!"

❖

The Interactive Walk

In contrast to a situation in which selectors have already made their decision and the selectee is left to respond, another approach brings the selectors and potential selectees into an exploratory walk together. The selectors start with an open slate and bring potential candidates into consideration through a variety of channels. People may have referred names to the selectors without the knowledge of the candidates. Selectors may have placed job opportunity listings in professional journals. The committee may have structured a confidential process whereby candidates could nominate themselves.

Selectors may gather names from a denominational database of eligible candidates.

This relational approach finds both selectors and selectees in a searching and discerning mode. Both parties are trying to match gifts and needs, graces and opportunities. Selectors and selectees come to the dialogue open to God's leading, with much uncertainty and awareness of the risks of rejection. Anticipate that God will use the interactive process to bring clarity to all participants. Discernment is not one-sided. As both parties practice discernment, each is affected. How can a selectee enter this process viewing it as a gift of the Spirit?

1. *Recheck your current calling.* The opportunity to make a move into a new role within an existing church or move to a different church may carry a certain romance and allure. But the Spirit may use this process to reaffirm the role in which you already serve. On the other hand, growing familiarity and comfort may lead to a plateau personally or for the institution. Look not only to your life journey but to the organization's life journey as well. Perhaps a new calling may arise within one's present setting for new vision and initiatives.

2. *Check your motives.* Is potential prestige getting in the way of seeking God's will honestly? Is affirmation of an invitation so strong that declining it seems impossible? Folks in one denomination tell the story of a seminary professor, trained for the pastorate, who came out of the pastoral ranks to his current position. Once every four or five years he allowed his name to be placed before several pastor search committees. When he became the final selection of one committee, he would say no to them and return to teaching. This repeating pattern signaled to him that he was still desirable and worthy as a pastor. That was all the affirmation he needed. But you see how this messy vehicle to affirmation used and abused the selection system and violated the integrity of the selectors and their process.

3. *Run the risk.* Engaging in an interactive relationship with a selection group calls for a high degree of openness and vulnerability. The dialogue does not come cheap. It is a work not only of grace but also of honest wrestling with the Spirit, a group of people, and one's own conscience. The stakes are high. It will call for self-death as well as self-fulfillment.

Chuck stumbled into a happy group of people when he was invited to lead a daylong leadership development event, "Doing Church Business the Worshipful-Work Way" (with special emphasis on spiritual discernment), for Grosse Ile (Michigan) Presbyterian Church. An interim pastor was closing out a three-year term following the retirement of a pastor of thirty-four years. The pastor search committee was about to inform the congregation of their selection for a new pastor. Throughout the seminar, as Chuck identified the ten movements operative within spiritual discernment, the members of the committee would attest to the validity of a particular movement from their own experience while working in the committee—providing a wonderful testimonial! Here is more of their story, told one year after the new pastor arrived.

WITNESS FROM SELECTORS
AND THEIR SELECTEE

Grosse Ile Presbyterian Church, Michigan
(as told by Ron Case, chair of the pastor search committee, and
by the Reverend Karl Travis, the new pastor)

The work of our pastor search committee was preceded by several important foundational processes. Even before our pastor of thirty-four years entered into retirement, a preliminary self-study group, which I chaired, was put in place to ask some basic questions. We began brainstorming the kind of intentional transition that would need to take place and what the nature of future church leadership. That work, along with the work of a search committee for an associate pastor eight years earlier, fed into our considerations.

A new interim pastor brought valuable insights from experience as a senior pastor, an interim pastor, and a pastor with conflicted churches. He also introduced us to a self-study process called Percept [developed by Percept Group, Inc., of California], and we welcomed the structure that it offered in contrast to our own floundering attempts at self-evaluation. The self-study group was tempted to pick and choose parts of the program but finally decided to do the whole thing. It would be thorough and time-consuming, a congregation-wide effort. We realized that God offers the best only when the people launch out in risk faithfully. This effort would be worthy of our commitment—and empowering.

The self-study group asked the session [governing elders] of the church to embark on the Percept program in order to better determine what kind of leadership we would seek. Despite speculation that a congregation-wide effort would not work and voices urging us to get on with a selection process, the congregation finally agreed to participate in the focus groups that would initiate the process.

For six weeks church members gathered on Monday and Wednesday evenings to consider a set of discussion themes.For the first time people engaged one another in matters of faith and opened themselves to God's leading for direction. We considered ourselves and the scriptural mission for the church. We reviewed demographic data to better understand the mission field to which we were called to serve. We were forced to look at ourselves in the context of community. Formerly church members related primarily to the pastor. Now we were relating to one another around important faith issues and confronting where we were and where God would have us be.

The data from the focus groups were shared with all participants and passed on to the session and deacons in a retreat, which was couched in musical, meditative worship styled after that of the Taizé community in France. We were determined to allow God to bring out the best in us. We felt empowered by the Spirit of God. We felt a sense of oneness. We took our final report back to the session for their embrace before passing it on to the congregation. This was not just another report to be filed away but had to become the primary agenda of the church. After approval, the report was dedicated at a worship service.

Finally the time came for the congregation to elect the pastor search committee. This step had been a long time coming in the eyes of some but was worth the wait. Two members of the self-study group were selected, including myself, and all others who were selected had participated actively in the focus groups. We were well aware of the process ahead of us. That process eventually led to preparation of the Church Information Form, which was sent to our denominational offices and made available to prospective candidates. That document honestly assessed who we were—both our strengths and our weaknesses.

As the committee entered into formation as a group, everyone involved took time to make certain important commitments. We committed to prayer, meditation, and reading of scripture, not only at the beginning of a meeting but any time we needed to stop for further prayer. Relationships would be important to our success as we adopted the concept of being the body of Christ in our very being. We valued the variety of gifts in the committee—including those of a sophomore in high school and a gentleman in his seventies who suffered deterioration from

Alzheimer's disease during our time together. We committed to a pastoral relationship with one another.

We welcomed suggested names of potential candidates from the congregation and others. We kept the congregation abreast of our process and progress.

In our relationship with the candidates we realized that we were on sacred ground. They were placing themselves in a vulnerable position, and we wanted to be a means of grace to them. We made a point of acknowledging every overture that they made with a written response on how we felt led to make a decision. Some of those decisions were hard, for several candidates felt called to us, but we did not see them as good matches. We did not want to blindside a candidate or the congregation, so we pulled no punches with the candidates regarding our weaknesses and our strengths.

Many of those same candidates complimented our utter candor. But we had to be equally honest with our own church leadership on the session. We reported to them some of the impressions of our church that the candidates had offered, taking responsibility for even delicate matters that arose. We did not want to dismiss or misrepresent the candidates' impressions.

A member of the congregation gave Karl Travis's name and phone number to our committee, saying he had experienced Karl's wisdom on a denominational committee related to stewardship. When I contacted Karl, he said he was not looking for a new position and was not interested. He did agree, however, to look over our Church Information Form and self-study. My first impression was that I had known him all of my life. He was open, affable, and responsive.

In a later contact Karl indicated that perhaps he had said no too quickly, for the church had been on his mind day and night. We stayed in touch, exchanging information and sermon tapes, and agreed to get to know each other better.

After a ninety-minute phone conversation between Karl and our whole committee, some magic began to operate, for we all immediately connected with him. Our Church Information Form impressed him in turn. It was solid and clear to him, and he was intrigued. We arranged for a visit.

That visit was like a building symphony for us. "Is this really us, or is God acting?" we asked ourselves. The experience was both troubling and exciting for Karl. He could not see how a call to our church would work out but could not bring himself to say no to it.

Next I represented the committee in a site visit to Karl's church in Roswell, New Mexico. When I walked into the church I immediately sensed love in the people's gracious welcome. Karl was the pastor, but he was one of them. I saw his leadership, which was evident in worship and the class that he taught. The people were comfortable with the concept and language of spirituality. I could hardly wait until I was on the edge of town to phone back my positive impressions to others on the committee!

Upon my return, I asked the committee, "Are we ready to decide?" We stepped back to pray and to talk seriously. That was one of the most powerful moments in my life: feeling that I—we—knew beyond a doubt that calling Karl Travis was right. Words could not describe what was happening. We were united in spirit as we gathered with our arms around one another. All we could say to God was thanks. Of course, we did find words to call Karl later and inform him of our decision and invitation to come.

A great deal of relief accompanied our announcement to the congregation. It had been a long process. Seeds of a crisis in confidence may have been sprouting. Some church members had wondered if we were selling the congregation short to prospective pastors, for surely all would have wanted to come right away.

When Karl came to our church, he requested permission from the session for our committee to stay together as a transitional committee. The Presbytery Committee on Ministry had some reservations about the idea but finally approved that plan. So we helped target special groupings of people for Karl to connect with early in his pastorate and to find ways to hear their stories. We also had a role in reminding the session and congregation of our self-study and how we needed to follow through on the three- to five-year goals we had named in the document.

Through this whole experience all the committee members grew in faith. And we miss one another. We were driven by God's direction, not our own tendencies. We came to understand that we cannot do God's work without God. We discovered that our role was to see God's work clearly.

Reverend Karl Travis is a graduate of Trinity University in San Antonio, Texas, and New College, the University of Edinburgh. He is a fourth-generation Presbyterian pastor who has deep roots in Texas and the Southwest. Here is his account of God's calling:

I suppose earlier in my ministry I was skeptical that the Holy Spirit was the prime mover in our call system. Given the technical and rather impersonal computer matching system in Presbyterian headquarters in Louisville, I wasn't sure the Spirit would get a word in edgewise. But I learned better. My first pastorate, a nine-year pastorate out of seminary, was a good match. Not long after I arrived there I knew sincerely that God wanted me there. And I wasn't looking to leave. In the fall of 1999 I received a phone call out of the blue from Ron Case. I did not have a Personal Information Form on file or in Louisville. I had not put out any feelers relative to a potential move. I was not looking, and in fact had turned down overtures from other pastor-seeking committees.

Ron asked if we could talk. I'm not sure to this day why I agreed, unless it was his reminder never to say no to God! But the thought of making a move across country to a different climate and culture was a stretch. I did enter into conversation—more to help them identify what they were looking for in a pastor than to engage myself. I made it clear that I was not looking.

What emerged from those conversations was awareness that the congregation had done some serious work. Members had engaged in the Percept process and had an excellent "revisioning" document in hand. They were honest about themselves—especially about their relative biblical illiteracy. They named their pocket of affluence on an island outside the city of Detroit as both a gift and a challenge. I had always seen affluence as problematic, so this caught my attention.

In our conversations I realized that this congregation was in search of a future, not just a pastor. The members realized that in their history they had become tied to a pastor and discerned that their faith needed to be nurtured with additional roots. They realized that they called for their confirmation classes to make faith statements but did not ask the same of adults.

The Percept process had taken them far from the corporate mind-set that was part and parcel of their culture. In that sense, the revisioning document was potentially controversial. I saw that those who had gone through the process—including the search committee—were on the same wavelength. But I feared that they might have run ahead of others in the church—even misrepresenting those who still operated out of the former culture.

The search committee said that the congregation wanted a preacher, teacher, and spiritual leader. (In retrospect I see that they also needed an administrator.) I began to move from serving as a consultant to them in their process to a personal engagement with them. I saw the depth of their honesty in the Percept documents. For me the aha! moment came when I asked the committee, "Why me?" Without our having spoken yet of stewardship—a favorite subject of mine—one member responded for the committee, saying, "We don't think that you can be bought off!" *Aha!* I thought, *the real issue for them is integrity in the midst of affluence!* (This had been understated in the Percept document.) I realized then that I saw their need and they recognized my gifts in ways that transcended their documents and our earlier conversations. Something mysterious was going on here.

A significant moment in my shift toward consideration of the position took place when I was invited to lead this group in prayer. Immediately I sensed a natural ease in sharing that prayer, an ease that had taken some time to develop with my former congregation. We were together in God! It was an honest, real, and sacred moment.

My actual yes came during Ron's visit to Roswell when he invited me to preach a candidating sermon at Grosse Ile. I felt it would be a betrayal of my faith family to respond immediately, so I talked with the committee later by phone about some of the specifics of the terms of the call. It all seemed so natural. We had experienced together this same ease at the initial interview and realized that coming to this agreement about the terms of call came about by more than coincidence.

There were other significant moments along the way. I had not known that Jesse [a member of the search committee] had been diagnosed with Alzheimer's. There was a time when something did not seem right with him, and I observed the committee's staying with him. They were so intentional about caring for him that I picked up the signal.

Another time I was asked a question about how I might handle a difficult situation in the church. I answered it my way, only to realize that I was answering a question they were not asking. We both felt inadequate and in need of grace.

My brother preached at my installation service. A member of the presbytery brought a guest, coincidentally in Detroit for the week, the bishop of Pretoria! His presence and blessing provided an additional sign for me that God was in this new match.

The culture of this church is one of expecting leadership to succeed. In the year since my arrival I have reevaluated "success." God brought me an important symbol in our move: for our furniture arrived late. Instead of going to a motel or to another home, we chose as a family to sleep in sleeping bags on the floor. It was a portent of future spiritual moments when I would experience barrenness rather than success. As a young pastor, the confirmation of my ministry had come with success. Those indicators are still present in this new situation, but they are now less consequential. In the midst of all the challenges, faithfulness is paramount. I continue to have the consolation of the Spirit of God that I am doing what I am supposed to be doing where I am supposed to be doing it. God called me here.

❖

The Community Way: Growing Leadership from Within

In a number of settings, a group of persons has the opportunity or responsibility to choose leaders from among its own membership. A board may need to elect legal officers. A small group may need to appoint a convener and leader. In recent years a number of Roman Catholic parishes have selected their pastoral council members through a discernment process that involves a large group of interested persons in selecting leaders—those who will serve on the council—from among themselves. Ellen has been instrumental in shaping this particular discernment process, which offers possibilities for any congregation that deems it appropriate to its situation.

In the early 1980s, twenty years after the Second Vatican Council opened the doors for more lay participation in the Roman Catholic Church, a number of parishes found themselves doing what they knew how to do from the corporate world—structuring the new entities of parish pastoral councils and finance councils as boards with business-as-usual agendas and the ordinary nomination/election/appointment ways of choosing membership.

During that same time some of the bishops in the American church began to notice what many called a "clergy shortage." Along with that naming came the opportunity to engage laity in leadership roles for pastoral administration in dioceses with rural populations and bishops who were ready. Women (members of religious communities) with administrative and pastoral experience and deacons (male) were the first to be called into these roles.

It didn't take long to realize that members of the local parishes could benefit from some serious formation—not just education— regarding the mission of the church and their role as the baptized in it. Ellen's book *Call to Leadership: Transforming the Local Church* reports her endeavors to form and educate parishioners in the Diocese of Great Falls–Billings, Montana, for their participation in the ministry of parish leadership. Later, as coordinator of leadership development in the Diocese of Kansas City–St. Joseph, Missouri, she brought this newly developed discernment selection design to the parishes of that diocese.

This unique design offers five education/formation sessions to an entire parish. The spiritual discernment process begins with those parishioners interested in further exploring their own call to ministry. They meet in a comfortable, prayerful space for as long as the process takes, and only when all are present do they (1) reflect further upon the present realities and future visions for their parish; (2) form a trusting, safe community for prayerful discernment; (3) name their own personal gifts, skills, qualities, strengths, and limitations; (4) become aware of the gifts, skills. qualities, strengths, and limitations of the other participants; (5) affirm all participants in the ministries that best use the gifts God has given them; and (6) prayerfully discern from among themselves the persons called to the ministry of the parish pastoral council (or other entity) at this time.

Each spiritual discernment session (a minimum of two hours) is laced with prayer, reflection on scripture (often the lectionary readings of the season), personal reflection, and sharing in groups of two or three as well as sharing in the whole group. One's personal motivations, sense of God's calling, the extent of personal/family commitments, relationship styles, and understandings of ministry are among the topics the groups explore. Rituals, guided meditations, music, and other art forms are interspersed throughout the process as appropriate and helpful to the participants. Participants may also be given short readings or exercises to do between sessions.

Each person in the group has a four-by-six card. At various times throughout the spiritual discernment sessions, participants use quiet time to write on these cards something they have noticed about other group members—such as a particular quality or an idea or question they want to pursue with someone. Periodically the group refers to these cards in the sessions, and eventually each participant receives the cards about him or her as part of the closing affirmation ritual.

After the community is formed and a level of trust has been developed, the group moves to discerning candidates for the council. Each participant lists on newsprint a core nucleus of persons with good gifts needed for current ministry (usually two to four), along with reasons for naming those individuals. Persons may not name themselves. This naming takes place in silence, and the pages are posted (in silence) for all to see. Conversation around the question "What do you see?" follows. If consensus surfaces on one or more names, those persons are asked if they would be willing to accept this invitation to be on a list of potential council members. The names of those who agree are listed on a separate piece of newsprint.

If there is no consensus, the participants are given the opportunity—after a few minutes of quiet reflection—to make one change on their list. Changes are appropriate only if someone has new insights as a result of the conversation or the silence.

The spiritual discernment continues via prayer, conversation, scripture reflection, song, card and newsprint writing (names and reasons) until consensus arises on the particular number of persons (the number was determined during the formation/education sessions) desired for the leadership roles (and one or two alternates, should a future need arise). At this time, the facilitator asks all whose names appear on the potential-candidates list whether or not they would be willing to accept this call to ministry. (There is still time to reconsider.) Following this process, the group worships together, praising God and affirming the gifts of every participant in the process.

This process—described in a nutshell here—may take weeks or even a few months. This kind of discernment has been a gratifying process in a number of settings; but as you can imagine, the setting and the process must match! Here are important considerations in determining whether this approach to discerning/selecting church leaders will work in your situation:

1. *The congregation must be patient about the outcome.* Finding common calendar dates is always a challenge. Stalemates in the process are unpredictable. You are counting on God's timing! You might need to plan ahead so that you can schedule formation/education sessions for two, four, or six months. These sessions can be discernment gatherings!

2. *The facilitator (discernmentarian) must be able to facilitate the process without partiality.* She or he works with the group to agree on ground rules and then facilitates the process without controlling the conversation or giving opinions. Being skilled as a spiritual director is important because the facilitator helps the group create a prayerful, trusting, and honest community.

   An outside facilitator is sometimes able to be more neutral and thus able to focus more on the process and the participants. But again the selection of the facilitator depends on the local situation. (You may want to reread the account of a pastor search process in chapter 4, in which discernment facilitators from one congregation led a process for a neighboring congregation.)

   In Roman Catholic parishes with which we've worked, the pastor or pastoral staff knew us, so they were able to invest their trust in the process and the facilitator. While some pastors were present, others chose to absent themselves for the actual discernment sessions. Whether present or absent, parish staff members need to be committed to and supportive of the discernment process.

3. *Be sure an appropriate space or room is consistently available for the group doing "worshipful work."* (A classroom next to a gym full of energetic basketball players just won't help!) Look for

a hospitable space, one that provides physical comfort, adequate room for movable groupings, and an environment suitable for worship.

If you embark on this particular spiritual discernment process, invite the parish-at-large or congregation to pray along with the group in discernment during its meeting times. In the past we've offered a small candle to every family or individual in the community, asking them to light it and offer a prayer for the group in discernment whenever it meets, for example every Tuesday night. Some congregations will offer a special prayer during each weekend worship service. However you include the congregation in prayer during the selection of its leaders, know that those engaged in the discernment will appreciate the support.

8

SPIRITUAL DISCERNMENT
IN VARIOUS SETTINGS

As part of preparation for writing this book, we developed twenty-three questions about selection processes for church leaders in congregational, judicatory, and denominational settings. Among other things, we wanted to know how potential candidates were identified and how they were introduced to the selectors. Carol Roth, a colleague in ministry, facilitated telephone interviews with knowledgeable persons in thirteen denominations using our questions.[1]

We are convinced that denominations, judicatories, and local congregations, regardless of their size and makeup, can be about the selection of leaders in more holy and wholesome ways than evidenced in our survey and experienced in our work with church leaders. We do not suggest throwing the baby out with the bathwater. Efficient and well-functioning systems exist within current search processes. We do believe that churches can build better leadership selection processes by relying more deeply on the age-old practice of prayerful spiritual discernment.

Having seen how spiritual discernment can inform a selection process, we are now ready to apply those insights to specific settings within congregational, judicatory, and organizational life. As you have been reading, you may have been trying to envision this process working in your church or religious organization.

Discernment within Different Church Polities

Let's look at three time-honored traditions of church polity, each defined by where final authority lies—especially in the arenas of ordination, clergy placement, property, and legal issues. The three traditions are *episcopal*—rule by bishops; *presbyterian*—rule by a presbytery (a geographically defined body consisting of an equal number of voting clergy and representative elders sent by their congregations); and *congregational*—rule by the local church. Each stream has looked to scripture for validation throughout history, but in recent times scholars have pointed out that scriptures actually reveal expressions of all three systems.

Our purpose here is not to show bias to any one form of church governance and polity but to show how the gifts and movements of spiritual discernment can function within each. We hold each tradition with respect. A common thread in all three forms for the selection process is communal discernment. Folks collaborate in each stream and in so doing are seeking the mind of Christ and the leading of the Spirit. The mechanics of reaching a conclusion or who finally names the conclusion are not as important as engaging in the process itself.

Many churches incorporate a mixture of all three traditions at various levels or stages of the selection process. Even though a particular church operates out of a particular tradition, it may lean or tend to operate in another's fashion. Congregationalists may lean toward presbyterian order, and Presbyterians may lean toward episcopal order, and so forth. So the lines of demarcation can become fuzzy.

In some settings the *episcopal* system may operate as an authoritative, top-down decision and implementation process, but most often it functions in a softer way as a community expresses oneness through the bishop as a sign of unity. The conciliar movement coming out of Vatican II and inherent in many traditions calls for councils of leaders at every level of the church to consider matters together. "It is highly desirable that in every diocese a special pastoral council be established, presided over by the diocesan bishop himself, in which clergy, religious [members of a religious order], and laity specially chosen for the purpose will participate. . . . In governing their dioceses, however, bishops have need of helpers and advisers, of priests especially to whom for that reason they should be glad to listen and even to consult."[2]

Wesley's advocacy of "holy conferencing" called people to meet together asking such questions as "How is it with your soul? And how is it with your calling?" The work of councils of bishops and other persons or groups engaged in an appointment system invites participants to consider together, which creates an opening for communal discernment.

WITNESS FROM A JUDICATORY
New England Jurisdictional Conference
The United Methodist Church

The New England Jurisdiction has taken a number of deliberate and intentional initiatives to introduce and practice spiritual discernment at every level of conference life. One of those initiatives relates to how appointments are made.

The appointment cabinet of the New England Jurisdiction of The United Methodist Church engages in a discernment process in appointment making. Initially the pastor-parish relations committees of local churches develop a profile of their church. Each pastor also has a profile. When a church becomes "open," the cabinet enters into a modified process of spiritual discernment as described by Danny E. Morris and Charles M. Olsen in *Discerning God's Will Together*.

Rooting. Every Appointment Cabinet meeting begins with worship that centers and prepares the group for the day's agenda. It is not unusual to spend an hour or more in worship at the beginning of each meeting. The bishop or district superintendents sometimes will select a specific scripture for reflection before entering into a time of discernment around a special issue or appointment.

Framing. The open church identifies the focus for discernment.

Grounding. We use a document called *Areas of Agreement for Appointment Making* as our guiding principles. The church profile also helps guide decision making.

Listening. Profiles of all of the pastors who must, should, or could move have been presented. The profile of the open church is shared. Questions are addressed. The cabinet enters into a time of silence. A spoken prayer is offered, followed by shared insights or observations.

Weighing. Names of pastors who meet the church profile are shared and listed on newsprint. The group moves through each name on the list and hears how that person fits the church profile. Only the positive aspects of the appointment possibility are raised. The second time the group moves through the list, members hear how persons may not fit the church profile. Questions and concerns lead to the elimination of some nominees. When more than one name surfaces as a good match, consensus is not reached, or appropriate names no longer remain on the list, the cabinet moves back into a time of prayer and listening. The group may need to hear the profiles again, revisit the guiding principles, hear a scripture, or return to prayer and repeat some of the discernment movements.

The group may determine it must "move beyond the map" and expand the possibilities to include additional names outside the guiding principles.

Discomfort regarding an appointment decision at the end of the cabinet meeting reopens the decision for future reconsideration.

When a name emerges as the best match, the process comes to closure.

While undergoing oral examination by members of the presbytery, Chuck was asked, "Who is your bishop?" He responded, "The brothers and sisters in the presbytery are my bishop!" That correct answer for Presbyterians passed! The *presbyterian* form of government places authority in the hands of a body of an equal number of clergy and lay commissioners, called the *presbytery* (or *classis* in the Reformed Church in America). Each session or consistory (group of ruling elders) from a congregation appoints elders in equal number to their clergy on staff to become part of that body. Then at every level of the church—presbytery, synod, and General Assembly—equal numbers of lay and clergy commissioners sit in deliberative session.

The pastor moderates the session and has final authority only to break a tie vote, if that is wise and necessary. Although the church has bought into a parliamentary culture that specifies *Robert's Rules of Order* as the guide for decision making at every level of the church, including the congregation and session, the pastor's role as moderator reflects a higher spiritual culture in the deliberative process. She or he can function as a discernmentarian who skillfully facilitates discernment at the session level. The deliberative table is seen as holy ground. Just as the pastor is given a significant place in the rites of baptism and Holy Communion, the rite of moderating the session brings the table of the board close to the Table of the Lord. The elders are not selected and set apart to represent the people but are elected by the people and ordained to lead—seeking the mind of Christ as they follow the will of God.

The important document from the constitution of the church, the *Book of Order*, outlines a high vision for the spiritual rootedness of elders and ministers. The preliminary principles assert that Christ is the Head of the church, that Christ calls the church into being, that Christ gives the church its faith and life, and that Christ is the church's sole authority. "It belongs to Christ alone to rule, to teach, to call, and to use the Church as he wills, exercising his authority by the ministry of women and men for the establishment and extension of his Kingdom. . . . In the worship and service of God and the government of the church, matters are to be ordered according to the Word by reason and sound judgment, under the guidance of the Holy Spirit."[3]

In the *presbyterian* system, the election of elders at the congregational level calls for selecting those spiritual leaders prayerfully. Also the calling of pastors invites a very intentional and spiritually rooted seeking. The pastor search committee, which the congregation elects, works in collaboration with the presbytery's Committee on Ministry. When the search committee's discernment of a new pastor is complete, the committee reports to the session, which calls a meeting of the congregation to vote on the nominee. When the motion to call the nominee is approved, the presbytery then votes to approve the call and the pastor is installed by the presbytery. Only the presbytery can install a pastor to a particular pulpit or declare it vacant.

The *congregational* form of government places the final authority in each individual congregation. The buck starts and stops there. But since making every decision in the context of a congregation-wide meeting is difficult, the congregational form has adapted to doing work in committees, ministry teams, and church boards. The wider associations have been constructed to provide common identity and resources for ministry of congregations in community, regional, national, and international mission.

Spiritual discernment in this context brings into play the three distinct types of prayer that Jesus practiced: (1) prayer in solitude—seeking to do one's own inner work of discernment; (2) prayer in intimacy—discernment in the company of a small group of persons where reality and "clearness" are sought; (3) prayer in assembly—discernment that hears the stories of the tradition and wider community. These three types of prayer are like a three-legged stool. Each leg is important but insufficient in its own right. The rungs that connect the legs are informing, interactive, and reinforcing. The selection process for the congregation must engage individuals in their own inner processes, engage groups together as they seek the guidance of the Spirit, and engage the congregation in its corporate life as it seeks to come to one mind.

Let's look at another witness from the episcopal tradition and then at guidelines prepared for churches in a congregational system. First here is an account from the Episcopal Dioceses of Connecticut about selecting a bishop suffragan (a bishop who assists the diocesan bishop) to work with Bishop Andrew D. Smith.

WITNESS FROM A JUDICATORY
The Episcopal Diocese of Connecticut

The Elections Committee continues to meet at least once a week in order to identify those individuals who possess the best combination of skills and traits to serve as bishop suffragan of the Diocese of Connecticut at this time in the diocese's history.

The committee's work has been largely that of a screening agent. While the committee used all practicable means available to make the position's availability widely known, including sending information packets to all bishops and posting the job description and nominating form on the diocesan Web site, committee members believed that their responsibility stopped short of recruiting candidates for bishop suffragan. They also believed that a person who is willing to be considered for election to bishop suffragan should be someone who discerns a call to that order of ministry rather than someone who is flattered or convinced by a persuasive phone call or letter.

After individuals submitted résumés and answered questions developed by the committee, the committee members reviewed each and every application. Objective data such as length of ordained ministry or time spent leading a parish were factors, as were more subjective factors such as nominators' comments and indications of spiritual strength. Each committee member came to the task with different weights on each of these indicators, although the committee as a whole had spent valuable time discussing which factors should bear on its decision.

After a great deal of prayerful consideration, the committee identified a group of individuals with whom to visit further. These conversations helped to flesh out the résumés and references in an important way.

Although objective matters continued to have some bearing on members' evaluations of the visits, also of importance were an applicant's spiritual discipline, ability to articulate the gospel, and network of emotional support. And there is that invaluable incarnational quality of presence: "Does this person have the personal presence to convey the good news of Jesus Christ to the people of the diocese?"

Since the bishop suffragan will have to work closely with and for Bishop Smith, the diocesan bishop, it is vital that each of the candidates has a chance to visit with him. Although Bishop Smith has stayed out of the details of the committee's work, he will review the prospective nominees before the slate is announced in order to determine that he could work with any one of them. His determination will be based, at least in part, on the results of this personal visit. In the case of nominees from outside the diocese, this encounter may be the only opportunity Bishop Smith has to meet with them.

The committee encouraged persons from throughout the Episcopal Church to consider nomination in this election and welcomed women and persons of color and/or nonmajority culture. After a process of conferring and discerning with the committee, the bishop offered a list of thoughts about experience and qualifications for the potential nominees:

- joy in the ministry of encouragement;
- proficiency in proclaiming the gospel in spoken and written word;
- discipline and creativity in prayer;
- personal life that exhibits the fruits of the Spirit;
- significant experience in parish mission, ministry, and administration;
- ability to clearly articulate and live a theology of baptismal ministry;
- openness to and appreciation of the breadth of life in the Episcopal Church;
- commitment to tithing and beyond;
- experience in youth ministries;
- exercise of responsible leadership in diocesan life;
- exposure to languages and cultures of the Americas and the Caribbean;
- small-church experience;

- leadership in issues of social witness and justice;
- demonstrated ability to provide for one's own nurture and well-being;
- a self-starter;
- experience and joy in serving in a multistaff ministry;
- a pastoral heart;
- ability to drive and freedom to travel away from home, sometimes for a week or more;
- enjoyment of a varied and demanding schedule;
- respectful of differences among people;
- computer literacy, fluency, and comfort.

The potential applicants were contacted and invited to offer preliminary input into the process: "We would like to get to know and appreciate you in a more personal way than that which normally comes across in résumés and professional profiles. Please share with us some reflections on your own life. Just a paragraph or two on whatever first comes to mind will be sufficient."

1. Please tell us about something you did, perhaps when quite young, that you did well, were proud of, and still feel good about.
2. Please tell us about something you are doing now—perhaps some new venture, cause, project or learning—that you especially enjoy or are excited about.
3. Please tell us about something new that you would like to test yourself in or tackle sometime in the future.
4. If there is something particular that caught your eye in our profile and/or job description, please comment.

A prayer was published in the diocesan newsletter, *Good News*, inviting prayer for and with the Elections Committee:

Most gracious Father in heaven, you have richly blessed us in our work these weeks past. You have brought before us men and women worthy of the challenges that face your Church in this place. And now as we move out to find your will among your faithful servants, continue to sustain us with the Holy Spirit. Bless us with humble hearts. Help us to set aside personal pride and self-seeking. Our need as a people and as a diocese you know far, far better than we. Teach us your way, Lord. Give us grace to be open always to the still, small voice of the Spirit, that you may be glorified in all that we do, Father, Son, and Holy Spirit, One God, now and forever. Amen.

Tara Hornbacker, in her teaching of practical ministry in a congregational system at Bethany Theological Seminary (Church of the Brethren), offers the following process for the selection of leaders:

It is important that a committee charged with selecting leadership, whether that be for a ballot or a slate or some other process, be attentive to the will of God and discerning God's call. The persons on the committee must be centered, and the work itself needs to be done in a worshipful manner rather than "book-ending" the meeting with prayer and devotions. Prayer and reflections are woven into the process. The committee should learn to think of the meeting as meeting for worship to consider calling leadership for annual conference. Worship is first and at the center, including times of silence. A proposed outline of such a meeting follows.

- Begin the meeting with a hymn, such as, "Move in Our Midst" or "Lord, You Sometimes Speak."
- Read slowly 1 Samuel 3:1-21 or Jeremiah 1:1-10.

- One person begins and reads very slowly, each person listening.
- When any one person in the group wishes some space or silence to ponder and speak out of the silence what the scripture is saying to them, they would simply speak out with "Stop, please."
- Give time for persons to respond and then the person who spoke "Stop, please" would resume the reading.
- From that point, reading resumes, again very slowly until someone else stops the reading for reflection. (This can take as much as a half hour.)
- Sing "Here I Am, Lord" quietly.
- Take at least ten minutes of silence to consider your own call to serve God.
- Share one-on-one the story of your call to your current ministry.
- Read John 13:1-17. Then ask questions like:
  "What are the issues we face as church today?" "What kind of leadership is needed for our church today?" "Who can lead the church forward into the reign of God, not just keep us from splitting?" "Who can inspire us to live out our lives as witnesses?"

  The answers to these questions are matters of discernment before you begin the calling process. We can little afford to fill slots with no concept of the connection to the actual call of God for us in those jobs.

Tara also draws upon the following questions, found in *Transforming Church Boards*, to help identify natural leadership:

To whom would you look or go in your congregation, district, and denomination—
- to fill you in on the history of the church or for background information on an issue?

- to assist you in bringing your vision into reality?
- to provide comic relief when the meeting gets tense?
- to pray with you over a specific concern?
- to figure out a difficult problem in the church?
- to encourage you if you were discouraged?
- to explore the biblical or theological insights on an issue or ministry?
- to assist you in resolving an interpersonal conflict?
- to listen when you want to talk and think out loud?
- other?

Discernment in Congregations

Since many readers begin leading at the congregational level, let's look more closely at variations in that setting now. A considerable amount of research and studies conducted in congregations explore the relationship between a church's size and its character. You may want to investigate the work of Carl Dudley, Lyle Schaller, or Arlin Rothauge in this arena. Rather than replicating their studies and wisdom, we want to focus our attention upon enhancing the selection process through spiritual discernment in a variety of size and style settings. Often the size of a congregation offers a clue to the manner in which the church selects, prepares, and deploys its leaders.

Arlin Rothauge, for example, sees four distinct sizes of congregations and designates them as *family*, *pastoral*, *program*, and *corporation* churches. In each size common threads of character and behavior are evident.[4] So we ask, How do the practices and movements of prayerful spiritual discernment interface with the significant differences in congregations?

In the early seventies, Project Base Church in Atlanta (an ecumeni-cal project of the Institute of Church Renewal) focused on training leaders for "base communities," small style-centered congregations, "underground churches," house churches, and small groups. We learned that style-centered congregations (new church plants that chose not to construct a building but to organize around a certain style of worship, mission, or common life) do not grow. Without a build-ing or a fully funded professional leader, such churches tended to expand rapidly to about thirty-five persons and plateau. Participants were enthusiastic about this vital cell of a living faith community, hardly keeping it a secret from others. They were often frustrated with their inability to grow beyond that threshold. "Why don't we grow, given how good this really is?" members asked one another.

Early in their genesis, these groups attracted able people, and mem-bers developed deep intimacy with one another, functioning as a sin-gle cell. Decisions were made by consensus. Leadership often was shared, and natural leadership was trusted as it emerged. A group developed its own set of stories and myths, a language of its own com-plete with humor, symbols, and informal rituals. The intimacy pro-duced a kind of "tribe," and visitors often felt left out, even though the group desperately sought to include them.

These groups were often powerful in their accomplishments—far beyond what might be expected from their numbers. They not only functioned as a committee of the whole but also implemented deci-sions with a hands-on approach. If a group's original "charism" was around advocacy for social justice, evangelism, engaging worship, intentional discipleship, or mission action, it was a formidable group.

Members of such groups had few hiding places. They knew one another well because they had moved through the stages of group formation together. In the early, "romance" stage, they thought, *How wonderful that we are so much alike.* In the disillusionment stage, they knew, *Goodness, how different we are from one another!* Finally they reached an accepting and functioning stage where they lived by grace and covenant. They knew one another, warts and all!

These "base communities" were generally start-up groups, and what we have learned from them is vitally important to our agenda related to selecting leaders. In many ways these groups were not different from the small, traditional congregations that have been in decline over the years in small towns and rural communities. Churches with fewer than thirty-five participants are like (and sometimes *are*) families. The former chair of our Worshipful-Work Board of Discerning Overseers, Dr. Ed Kail, specialized in small-church ministries while on the faculty of Saint Paul School of Theology. He describes the very small church in the following way:

> Leadership roles are informal, so the selection process is informal as well, shared in mutual discussion. Folks who have institutional memory tend to have heightened influence. Family connections of honor, deference, and performance come into play. People are able to tolerate personal flaws and idiosyncrasies. They recognize potential leadership even when it has not been demonstrated in the church. A leader may be named in order to grow into the role in an organic development. Visiting or temporary pastors may fill the pulpit but are outsiders and have little influence in the way decisions get made. Only when a high trust level has been developed can a little influence be exercised.

In this setting of family, intimacy, community, and trust, how can leadership be named and blessed via spiritual discernment rather than through a secular powwow or family fight? "Worshipful work" is a theme that pervades everything we do and advocate in church leadership, administration, and governance. The theme seems appropriate in the single-cell setting—even where there is no formally structured selection group or process.

Here are some suggestions: Introduce worship and prayer into the current informal contexts of discussion related to leadership. The leadership role may be temporary, lasting only a week or a month or defined by a specific task. In any event, ask, "On whom is God's Spirit resting for this function?" Introduce a brief time of silence as parentheses within the discussion—whether that discussion is in the parking lot, in the kitchen over coffee, before or after the church service.

A student in one of our seminary classes reported that members of his small rural congregation gathered on cold mornings around the potbellied stove located to one side of the sanctuary before church services began. He was struck with the quality of caring and amount of communication that took place in that location and was tempted to hold the worship service there. But his parishioners insisted on moving to their traditional places in the pews when the worship service was about to begin! The integration of worship and work may provide an opening to engage in discerning listening and even in biblical reflection in opportune informal settings. Look for those openings and moments!

Another option is to bring the selection discussion into worship. The services tend to be informal anyway. Why couldn't the discernment happen there as well? People might be more comfortable engaging in prayer related to a specific need and task. You could celebrate a positive response from a selectee and secure a public covenant.

In the Quaker tradition discernment is the norm. Meetings are called "Worship for Business." Some meetings fill positions via a process such as the following:

- Present a job description.
- Observe a time of silence.
- Voice names for consideration.
- Ask people if there are any unknowns and request information as to who the one named is and why the name was given.
- Take time to worship.
- Raise name(s) again. (Often there is only one.)
- If more than one name is raised, ask those offering the names to say why they support those individuals.
- Repeat the process.
- Delay the decision until later if more than one name is voiced.

Quakers teach the Worship for Business form to children as young as fourth graders as well as to youth and adults who come into the church. The clerk of each meeting also models it.

Although variously sized gatherings may use this model, it particularly offers clues as to how a small worshiping congregation could select leaders in the context of worship. The formality could be streamlined, so that the process flows in a manner consistent with a congregation's informal style.

THE SPINAL-CORD CONGREGATION

When a single-cell faith community will not or cannot give up its operating style, its growth is impaired. But many groups do make a transition into growth, and with growth comes the necessity of operating in multiple groups that somehow relate to one another. Strategists in new-church development insist that a clear vision of what the church is to become is important from the beginning. If you want to start a single-unit, rugged, mission- or style-centered congregation, plan to start a small church. But if you want to grow a large church, plan to start a large church from the beginning. Think multiple cells.

What can the connecting link among groups be? The mechanism for connecting multiple cells is the central nervous system, a network that both sends and receives messages to and from the brain. We will call a congregation seeking to connect cells the *spinal cord congregation*. Rothauge speaks of a *pastoral size* congregation. It tends to be small to medium in size. While not seen as the brains of the church, the pastor is a central entity in an initiation-and-response system. The pastor is located in a pivotal position. Pastor and people are called into a covenant relationship. If a spinal cord is damaged or severed or if there is impairment in the brain and its functions, the community will suffer paralysis, being unable to function as a healthy body.

Decisions made in this system involve pastoral participation. This fact does not imply that the pastor always knows best or has the first and last word in all matters. The pastor may in fact function as a skilled facilitator of a decision or selection process. In the United Methodist system, for example, the pastor chairs the nominating committee. In the Presbyterian/Reformed system, the pastor is the moderator of the board of elders and conducts the meetings.

Trusting relationships are vital. In some way this kind of congregation is a charismatic system that roots deeply in the gifts and persona of the pastor. The deeper the trust, the more latitude is given to initiate and propose. Likewise a pastoral listening ear and heart, coupled with wise and good communication, can enable the body of individuals and multiple cells to function together.

The connection to the larger church, regardless of the denomination's polity, will be channeled through the pastor. She or he is a creature of a heritage of faith and has been formally trained in theological seminary to function within a given denominational system. The pastor bears the institutional story and interprets its current vision and mission agenda, which will be brought into the mix of the congregation's own process of vision and mission strategy.

In any family and emotional system, how one defines oneself becomes critical to the health of the organization. A pastor may define herself or himself as a friend to all, as the resident biblical scholar/theologian, as the CEO of a corporation, or as the shepherd who feeds the flock. To engage the congregation in spiritual discernment, the pastor will need to define herself or himself as "spiritual leader." Unfortunately, some old models of theological education have not prepared pastors to assume this primary identity. The integration of spirituality into leadership needs to be defined, modeled, and practiced in the heart and soul of the pastor. In many ways the pastor will come to see himself or herself as a spiritual director—not only to individuals in one-on-one settings but to the congregation as a whole.

The pastor and the congregation need to attend to the inner movements of spiritual formation in order for spiritual discernment to take root as a culture. Let us highlight three inner movements that call for attention: (1) The movement of *letting go* or relinquishment invites people to surrender and open themselves more and more to the love and will of God; (2) The movement of *taking hold* invites people to assess their respective callings and vocations and to care about what matters to God; (3) The movement of *naming God's presence* invites people to look into their individual and collective stories, where they can name and celebrate God's presence in their midst. The pastor as spiritual director will tend these movements in her/his parish/parishioners.

For several years Worshipful-Work has conducted leadership training events called "Schools for Discernmentarians." When people first hear the term *discernmentarian*, they wonder how hokey this training event might be. But when they have had an opportunity to sit with the idea, they realize that if a *parliamentarian* is helpful to a group operating within parliamentary culture, one who gifted in the process of spiritual discernment can rightfully be called a *discernmentarian*! We find that both pastors and lay leaders can claim this new identity and function within it. They begin to redefine their own ministry, pulling together a wealth of past experience and giftedness, while allowing a new identity and call to coalesce around a central pole of discernment. They begin to glimpse a new vision and a commitment that signal their availability to work with others in facilitating discernment. New life and intent flows from this redefinition!

The key to selecting leaders in the small- to medium-size church, where the pastor is vitally engaged in that system of stimulation and response, lies with each pastor. If the pastor has been trained in a leadership model around a limited management, theological, liturgical, or shepherding design, retooling may be necessary. But if the pastor self-defines as a spiritual leader, is cognizant of the movements of spiritual discernment, has earned the trust of the people, and has deep relational capacities, these assets will more likely open a congregation to the prospect of selecting their leaders via spiritual discernment.

A BIBLICAL WITNESS

from Peter, James, and John, Selectees
(based on Mark 9:2-8; 14:32-42)

The three of us were not just Jesus' "teacher's pets." But his relationship to us and ours to him suggested something profound about Jesus' leadership style. Sure, he was a magnificent teacher among the large crowds. Yes, he was a wise and skilled debater with his adversaries. And when he shared with the Twelve, he had a great knack for relating our day-to-day experience with the tradition of the faith of Israel. But he also had this quality of inviting us to share with him in the intimate moments of his life—moments of both ecstasy and despair.

Jesus selected and invited the three of us to pray with him. One time we went to a remote mountain where his connection to the prophets Moses and Elijah was so real and intense that God's very presence and glory encompassed him. And we were there! He invited us into it! (And our vanity almost destroyed the moment!) On another occasion he selected us to go with him into the loneliness of a secluded garden to stare down the face of death. We were so tired and confused by all the hubbub in Jerusalem over his claim to kingship that we fell asleep. We woke to his agony as he prayerfully faced God with the plea to let this cup of suffering pass from him. And we were there! He invited us into it!

In the days following his crucifixion, resurrection, and ascension, we have been pondering the meaning of these experiences with our brother and sister disciples. They honored our special role, realizing that Jesus must have intended to demonstrate that leadership is relational, that extreme ecstasy or painful agony does not limit leadership's bounds. He prepared us all by allowing us to feel and see his heart and soul as well as his body and mind. Our task remains to integrate the same into our own witness and leadership.

THE EXTENDED-LIMB CONGREGATION

When a church reaches a size where a pastor no longer can manage everything in a central nervous system model, more persons and groups assume responsibility for the program and mission life of the congregation. Committees, small groups, organizations, and task groups emerge. In the new system, visioning, planning, decision making, accountability, communication, implementation, and evaluation are necessary. We will designate it *extended-limb congregation*. Rothauge calls this type of church the *program church*. The congregation develops arms and legs through which it can express its mission. The program is conducted by teams of lay members who engage in a variety of ministries according to their gifts and callings.

The pastor's leadership remains important, but the leadership style needs to change. A potential source of frustration, both for the church and for the pastor, often arises when a pastor who has been schooled in and has practiced effectively in a spinal-cord church continues to operate in the same manner in an extended-limb church. The pastor's role remains vital, to be sure, but in a different way. The extended-limb church calls for a more collegial style, an understanding of systems, and a posture of permission granting. Trying to pass everything through the pastor will overload the nervous and emotional circuits, thereby burning out both the pastor and the people.

Since the extended-limb congregation is a working church, the members who find themselves in leadership personally engage in the planning or conducting of the ministries. These churches tend to organize with a number of standard committees—often suggested by the denomination's guidelines. Chairpersons of committees usually sit on the church council or board, where they become guardians and protectors of a mission area—"turf"—especially where budget, limited volunteers, and communication resources are allotted.

The committees also tend to be organized according to "religious oughtness" rather than functional activities. For instance, since the church *ought* to do worship, there is a worship committee. Since the church *ought* to be a friendly community, there is a fellowship committee. Since the church *ought* to grow in the faith, there is a nurture/education committee, and so on. Internally the church needs to support staff, manage finances, and care for the building, so committees form and attempt to mesh their work into the program committees. A mechanistic organization with a sophisticated organizational chart often emerges. Recruiting leaders can become an exercise in filling slots to satisfy the organization or denominationally suggested positions. This task necessitates a nominating committee with a sufficient number of warm bodies to fill the slots, matching gifts, education, and life experience with the needs of the committees.

Can a congregation conduct a selection process at a deeper spiritual level in such an environment? Try this for starters: Invite each committee or organization to identify its calling and to name the spiritual leadership qualities that members would like to see new participants possess. If the congregation conducts comprehensive gifts/interests/calling identification, some matching can begin, but that is only the starting point. Encourage folks to apprentice with the committees that interest them or at least to visit several consecutive meetings. Often new leadership will emerge from within a ministry itself. When contacting potential new leaders for committees and boards, be honest with them about other related duties or meetings that go with the territory. Some council members have told us that they were members of their church council by default—meaning they said yes to one invitation only to discover that it automatically placed them in four additional leadership constructs that held meetings and carried responsibilities.

Many churches are moving away from a rigid, complicated organizational chart reflecting a mechanistic understanding of organizations to a more organic and fluid model. Programs, initiatives, and mission extension happen only in response to the calls or visions of the church members. If no one has the vision or calling, no ministry is initiated.

New understandings about how small groups form and develop lend credence to this strategy for the extended-limb church. Rather than structure programs around religious "oughtness," train group leaders and participants in fundamentals of small-group dynamics. In other words, invite each mission group to incorporate the marks of worship, fellowship, nurture, and mission into its life. Or you might consider schooling each participant in the four Worshipful-Work practices of story, reflection, vision, and discernment.

In the extended-limb model, training and support are essential. Any group's connection with the congregation as a whole will materialize when the group's stories are expressed in corporate worship, its projects are supported financially, and its mission is communicated and interpreted in the news channels of the church. These expressions invite the larger community to celebrate these stories and the evidence of God's presence in them. Moreover, the whole church can focus on each group's struggles and needs.

The discerning eye in an extended-limb church will try to spot potential leaders emerging from within small groups. Naming, encouraging, and putting these individuals in relationship with a spiritual mentor within the congregation can grow new leaders. A high priority for the pastor may be equipping leaders to understand group formation, relational leading, and the practices of a prayerful group life.

Organizing through clusters of groups for ministry rather than for a theological oughtness model will necessitate a new way of forming the church board. The board members will be selected for their capacity to oversee the whole church and its multiple ministries. Then they will share and model spiritual leadership in their own life and meetings. These effective spiritual leaders will be like angels to their church.

The letters to the seven churches in Revelation are each addressed to "the angel of the church." What or who are these angels: guardian angels in the mystical ecology of heaven? the ethos or personality of the congregation? Or might the "angel" be the group of elder leaders in each church, symbolically represented as "stars" in the right hand of Jesus (Rev. 1:20)? They were to have ears "to listen to what the Spirit was saying to the churches" (Rev. 3:22).

A BIBLICAL WITNESS

from the Angel of the Church in Laodicea, Selectees
(based on Revelation 3:14-22)

Whoever thought that we would be called an *angel*? But that is what the living Lord called us. We are a small group of elders in the church at Laodicea, chosen because of our wisdom and maturity in the faith. We were respected and trusted. In many ways we reflected the personality or ethos of our congregation. We thought that our little church was doing just fine—in fact, very well. We were rich and had prospered, being unaware that we needed anything.

Then one day a letter came to the church simply addressed to "The Angel of the Church of Laodicea." It was passed on to our elders' meeting and we opened it. We sensed that we were the "angel" of the church and that we were stewards of the spirit and life of the congregation. The letter concluded that we had better have ears to hear what the Spirit was saying to the churches! (We later discovered that six other churches had received similar letters—all tailored to their own situation.)

We were confronted with our lukewarmness, being neither hot nor cold. We were told that we were blind to the spiritual lethargy in our midst and that we needed to have new eyes to see how things really were. Suddenly we knew that this letter was from a living Lord Jesus and that he was standing at our door knocking—waiting to be allowed in. If we would only let him in he would stay and eat with us at an intimate table.

In living with this letter, we came to grasp that our duty as leaders was not just to create a rich, comfortable house of ease.

We were to be spiritual leaders who could see reality through the eyes of Jesus. We were to minister to the spirit and heart of the church, testing its temperature and providing the kind of oversight to ensure that our little church would be a church of vital, active, and alive faith. The one who called us into being and wrote this letter wants to live in our midst!

❖

THE FULL-BODY CONGREGATION

The largest churches are often a law unto themselves. They may have denominational connections, but they do not need the denomination to survive and engage in ministry. Large, independent megachurches reflect many of the same characteristics as the large denominational churches. Our designation of these congregations as *full-body churches* suggests that they include the small cells, sophisticated and complex nervous system, extended limbs, *and* the capacity to function on their own. Rothauge calls this fourth type the *corporation church*.

These churches usually employ large staffs, including a mix of professional clergy and lay specialists. The paid lay specialists may be full- or part-time—often having grown into leadership from congregational participation. The top staffers are often well schooled in the theories of management and organizational development.

The church board or council is not a large table of program committee chairs but a small table of wise persons who are selected for their ability to give oversight to the whole. Teams of both paid staff and lay leaders attempt to operate in a collegial style as they guide the programs. The staff brings sophisticated and extensive training to leaders at every level.

Programs are most often driven from the bottom up, that is via a process of listening, assessing needs and gifts, and a shared visioning process. These churches intend to free up and allow the ministry of the laity to unfold and therefore are generally permission-granting. The staff helps to connect gifts and needs, trains leaders, assists in communication with the whole system, and accesses both financial and other resources for the ministries. Church members are encouraged to be involved in small groups for personal spiritual growth and accountability. These groups become the seedbeds for new crops of leaders.

Study and educational opportunities are regularly offered—often resembling a lay seminary in system and content. Some churches include opportunities for spiritual direction and schooling in the disciplines of the faith. For persons with special needs or circumstances, support groups offer solace, insight, and companionship.

These churches *intentionally* welcome visitors, invite them back, and graft new people into the life of the church—often via small-group life and discipleship classes. Worship includes efforts to be "seeker friendly."

As we look at the task of selecting leaders for these large churches, we ask, What kind of corporation church is it? If the full body church reflects an organic system, then the selection process will not be confined to finding the right person for the spot but will seek the right spot for the person. The process will be ongoing, not limited to a nominating season of the year. Begin with a constant process of listening to the hearts and yearnings of people both inside and outside the church. Help people formulate their own faith-journey stories. In those stories look for patterns or twists that reveal where and how God is present and calling. Look for gifts. Enable people to sit with a yearning, holding it patiently before God awaiting God's timing. Allow "clearness groups" to help individuals discern their calls. Network and link together those with common needs or visions. Free them and encourage them, while praying with and for them.

In this model, the selecting team operates more like yeast in a loaf of bread than workers in a production line. The work is not always neat and clean. Some exceptions become the rule. The Spirit works in surprising ways!

A BIBLICAL WITNESS

from Eldad and Medad, Selectees
(based on Exodus 18; Numbers 11:24-29)

Poor Moses, he had really been under a lot of pressure. Once we crossed the sea to the safety of the desert, the people began to grumble. Problems arose. Of course, folks went to Moses for judgment and were wearing him out. But no one dared say anything to Moses about the obvious stress for they owed him a great debt of gratitude after all.

Then one day Moses' father-in-law, Jethro, came for a visit. We could see the depth of their regard, affection, and trust for each other. Jethro observed what we had seen in Moses, and he leveled with him, suggesting that Moses divide the throng into smaller units and appoint elders to serve and judge with him. Jethro said, "You will surely wear yourself out, both you and these people with you" [Exod. 18:18]. His wisdom became a lesson in shared leadership. We were selected, along with others, to be leaders.

One day Moses invited the seventy leaders to the tent where God shared God's Spirit with all of the elders as well as with Moses. But we were not there. We were, in fact, doing our chores and taking care of people back in the camp. Somehow God's Spirit fell upon us. They prophesied at the tent, and we did the same in the camp. Some folks were alarmed, for we seemed to be operating outside of normal expectation and tradition. They went to Moses and pleaded with him to stop us. But Moses responded, "Would that all the Lord's people were prophets, and that the Lord would put his spirit on them!" [Num. 11:29].

That affirmation, blessing, and encouragement freed and empowered us to do God's work and proclaim God's presence in corners of the camp where prophecies made in the tent would never be heard. We discovered that trusting all of the laity and granting permission to follow God's call are keys to being "a kingdom of priests!"

❖

Spiritual Discernment at Other Church Levels

THE DENOMINATIONAL JUDICATORY

In the early nineties, while we focused on leadership at the church board level, Loren Mead, founder of The Alban Institute, asked us if we knew of any judicatories that were working well. That question was not on our radar at that time. A colleagues made a prediction: "When laser technology was being developed, they envisioned only a limited number of applications for it. But look at the uses to which we put that technology today—scanning the prices on our groceries, communications, surgery, et cetera. We have focused on the integration of spirituality in administration and governance at the local church board/council level and have developed a model based on accessing the practices of faith at that level. But I predict that this model will have an equally profound effect in mission groups, church staffs, judicatory structures, and in the councils and working teams of major denominational life." He was right! Over a five-year period, commencing with the formation of Worshipful-Work in 1995, an increasing amount of consultation, leadership development, and experimentation has taken place in judicatory settings.

Folks who volunteer their time and energy in denominational structures have the same yearning for their experience that lay church members have about the way they meet, interact, and finally decide in congregational settings. They want those meetings to be inspirational and life-giving—a location for meaning making! Judicatory leaders ask, "How can we elevate the character of our life together beyond parliamentary rules, striving, debating, and often the resulting impasse?"

Judicatory by judicatory, people are trying to reclaim the high ground of faith practices in planning and administration. Changing old models and paradigms is not easy. People do what they know how to do. One United Methodist pastor in the middle of an annual conference rose to object, "Why are we trying to utilize a method of discernment that is strange to us, when we have been schooled in parliamentary procedures for years? This is confusing and a waste of our time. Let's go back to the way that we all know. After all, it works for us." Those remarks drew a chorus of responses from others—a number of them women and younger leaders—who said, "It works for you, but it does not work for us!"

For the past five years, Worshipful-Work has convened a series of annual collegiums titled "The Practice of Spiritual Discernment in Decision Making in National and Regional Religious Bodies." An ongoing learning community has been forming as each body presents case studies of initiatives to transform its own decision-making culture.

When looking at the selection process for placing both clergy and lay leaders in judicatory systems, one sees the tie to organizational culture. Sometimes leaders in our judicatory systems do not know how to access or timidly access the practices of their faith traditions for the ordering of their common life and mission. We call upon all judicatory leaders to look at their spiritual heritage, activate the practices inherent in their own charism, and live deeply into them, rather than trying to borrow the latest management scheme from the world of the social sciences.

When the culture of the whole begins to change and spiritual discernment becomes a way of life, the results will impact the judicatory in a profound way—especially in its selection of leaders.

WITNESS FROM A JUDICATORY
The Synod of Southeast Michigan
Evangelical Lutheran Church in America

Bishop Robert Rimbo was introduced to the practice of spiritual discernment and the Worshipful-Work model in a conference for pastors of large churches. Then a local pastor, he realized the value of applying this practice and this model in the local congregation. But soon after that conference, he was elected bishop in his church, which caused him to raise the question "What might spiritual discernment look like if it were practiced in the context of a synod's structure and operation?"

One of Bishop Rimbo's first challenges as bishop was to fill a staff position that would carry a portfolio for justice issues, ethnic-minority ministries, and ministry with small, struggling inner-city churches in Detroit. He introduced spiritual discernment to a search committee, and the members began their work, resolving to practice spiritual discernment in their process. They learned that they needed to go much deeper into the meaning and practice if it were to be an authentic journey. They read about spiritual discernment and invited an outside facilitator at critical junctures in the process. They engaged scripture. They mined and claimed their own story—especially of their own transition from relating to the bishop in an organizational style to a more collaborative style.

Along the way the search committee discovered that simply selecting a staff person and putting him or her into the current operative box would lead to frustration. The discernment led committee members to consider the whole culture in which staff operated in distinct boxes and how new understandings of staff resourcing for congregations might change the operation. How could they work as a fluid team in response to emerging visions and needs?

The committee also recognized that a cultural shift into discernment would affect the structure and conduct of the annual synod meeting. The initial question—"Who should be selected for leadership to a particular position?"—led the group down a path of profound institutional transformation, which is still in process!

RELIGIOUS ORGANIZATIONS

The proliferation of parachurch and ecumenical not-for-profit religious organizations in recent years has added some imposing structures to the religious landscape. Religious not-for-profit organizations now are important players on the religious scene. Whereas references to the "ecumenical" arena formerly suggested interaction among official denomination groups, today these boundaries are being stretched. Ecumenical networks and associations rise out of common vision and need. We are tempted to write an article titled "How the Parachurch Stole the Ecumenical Movement"! A look at comparative budgets, educational programs, consulting engagements, mission initiatives, and influence would make for interesting comparisons.

It is crucial that these organizations behave and conduct their business in a manner that brings credit to the religious mission they espouse. Since their boards of directors tend to be self-perpetuating rather than elected and selected by a larger membership, these organizations may welcome the gift of spiritual discernment. Prayerfully framing and sitting with the selection of successors can reap a great harvest. Not doing so may leave the organization vulnerable to increasingly entrenched leadership that tends to protect its power. When and how will the organization secure new leadership? What emerging mission and strategic directions should the organization undertake? And what kind of new board members will be needed?

One creative approach to board development reframes the fixed-term model. A more fluid model asks, What is the next developmental step that our organization needs to take? Then the board selects new members to serve on the board and facilitate the stated goal. Board members' terms may be measured in years or in months, depending on the nature of the organization's current initiatives!

The listening and shedding movements in spiritual discernment are especially important for self-perpetuating boards. Faithfulness may call for relinquishing control. Voices on the edge and outside the ministry need to be heard to see where God is already at work. Knowing where those edges of energy lie provides a key element in the search for those whom God is already calling into the work—who are being identified and finally selected.

RELIGIOUS COMMUNITIES

Members of Roman Catholic apostolic religious communities publicly commit themselves to a distinctive way of following Jesus Christ. It is a way of life beyond a professional lifestyle, and it is a way of life defined by choices the members make about their relationship to

God, to one another, to possessions, and to all of creation. These choices have an internal coherence and consistency: They imply prayer, ministry, celibacy, and a commitment to the common visions, priorities, and the charism of the particular community. Collaboration with other persons who share the desire to live wholesome Christian lives is a daily reality in their ministries, and this shared purpose helps animate and shape their mission.

Women's and men's religious congregations, both monastic and apostolic—of family, pastoral, program, and corporation size—have practiced spiritual discernment in matters of congregational mission, choice of individual ministries, and in the selection of leadership for many years, and in some cases, centuries. Nevertheless, they have never been and are not now immune to the social and cultural matrix around them, and so at any time they may take on—or let creep in—the strengths and limitations of that matrix.

Religious communities, being human, can be led or can resist leading by the Spirit. Some community members may prefer a high level of public debate on all issues, including the selection of leaders; others see a patient process of spiritual discernment as worth the effort. Communities can have an almost unsinkable optimism about their future, or they can resist the discipline of making hard choices, setting definite directions, and clarifying mutual expectations. Communities can become caught up in the materialism that our culture feeds its citizens via sophisticated technology. Religious communities can refuse the struggle to integrate personal freedom and corporate identity, mimicking the strains on family life that threaten the fabric of society. Without personal and corporate discernment, community members can search desperately for a job, then reluctantly accept work unsuitable to their personal talents. Religious congregations can decide to step back from collaborating with other congregations in speaking their truth to the hierarchical church. They can choose to pay so much attention to their governance structures that they become paralyzed in mission. In short, religious communities are, by virtue of their degree of attentiveness to God's Spirit, choosing to move toward extinction, minimal survival, or newness of life.

Religious communities that intentionally practice spiritual discernment touch the very Spirit of God. Their encounters with God are revelatory, leading to a renewed understanding that their community is a part of God's unfolding story. Such experience promotes reverence for the value of mutuality and communal choices.

A phrase commonly used among religious community members, one that illustrates a penetrating understanding of our relationship with God, is *ongoing formation*. This phrase does not imply a break with the past but a reawakening—a drawing upon God for fresh insight into dependence on God. Wearing the mantle of ongoing formation is a way of affirming that God is enough, that God is everything. Far from fostering a privatized spirituality, ongoing formation calls people to be seized by God and caught up in commitment to the demands of the gospel. It calls persons to conversion, which in turn leads to openness to a variety of choices. And good choices are at the heart of renewing religious congregations.

The larger and more geographically spread a religious community is, the more creative the congregation must be in order to involve all its members in choices that affect the entire community. Some common issues related to selection of leaders are the following:

1. involving members in the process;
2. judging value of electronic communications versus face-to-face meetings;

3. creating a timetable that allows for individual, small-group, and large-community dialogue and discernment;
4. developing and making available common resources for the process, for example, historical documents, worship texts;
5. mapping and synthesizing where community members are in the process;
6. addressing any political elements that appear to be creeping into the process; and
7. finding the pros and cons of a community members' facilitating the process.

Ellen's religious community of one thousand members engages in an extensive discernment period every four years for the selection of a president and two vice presidents. Everyone in the community is invited into reflection, prayer, and dialogue.

WITNESS FROM A
RELIGIOUS COMMUNITY
The Sisters of Charity, BVM

A common prayer is prayed daily. The leadership needs of the evolving congregation are a topic for conversation at dinner tables and geographical gatherings, and the answers to questions for personal reflection about one's own gifts and capabilities are shared. Eventually everyone in the community is welcome to send five invitation cards to persons they wish to invite into personal discernment regarding the leadership positions. (The invitations read: "Trusting in the Spirit . . . I invite you to consider a leadership position . . . for the following reasons. . . .")

After about two months have elapsed, those sisters who have received a significant number of invitations choose whether or not they wish to enter into a weekend of further discernment with other sisters who likewise have a significant number of invitations. That weekend is followed by a community-wide mailing, in which those sisters choosing to continue on in the process give written responses to significant questions, such as: "Three major priorities for the congregation over the next five years are . . . ; I describe my personal leadership style in the following way . . . ; I bring the following strengths to a leadership position . . . ; I would need the following talents and skills of others to complement my own. . . ."

The discernment for selection of leaders then continues in a weeklong process with the final candidates and about forty elected members of the congregation. That process varies but includes prayer services, individual and small-group reflection, presentations, and fishbowl exercises (in which the larger group listens to a conversation by several participants). The discernment time concludes with the formal balloting required by canon law.

These learnings could have universal application:

1. In the long run, religious communities actually strengthen their unity when their members are honest in conversations.
2. As congregations move through a shifting and changing milieu, they need to cling tenaciously to the bedrock (the charism) upon which their lives are built, to keep calling themselves back to the basics.
3. In selecting leaders, a religious community needs to be poor enough in spirit to relinquish the security of the past and to weed out less essential components in the process itself.
4. Communities should realistically assess the challenges that lie ahead for their leaders.
5. Know that communities can make mistakes, even after prolonged discernment.

6. Keep telling your story. If your founders were founding or reforming your congregation today, how would they assess the world as it cries out for proof of the presence and providence of God? Then what would they do?

Johannes Metz wrote in a 1978 book: "We [religious communities] need to continue to press for the uncompromising nature of the Gospel and of the imitation of Christ. In this sense we are the institutionalized form of a dangerous memory within the Church."[5] Be open to the overwhelming power of God's Spirit—the fire and driving wind—to inform your choices.

AFTERWORD

Moving toward a Culture
of Spiritual Discernment

When you honestly compare your current decision-making and selection modes to an alternative path of communal spiritual discernment, you may realize that you have a long way to go. But the path has some clear markings. It is not an uncharted quagmire. How might you position your community to move into that new path?

Continue to claim the mystical wedding of "seeming good to the Spirit" and "seeming good to us." Reclaim the age-old practices and disciplines that will open your community to God's word and spirit. Just as a good coach who faces the ineffectiveness of a losing team returns to the fundamentals of the game, religious leaders can return to fundamental practices that root and ground the selection process. The effect of that return will be life-changing, leading to nothing less than the conversion of the church.

How does a faith community move intentionally and strategically into that future around the pole of "seeming good to us"? Cultural shifts seldom happen as a result of grand schemes that are detailed and comprehensive in nature. Most shifts happen when a small group of dedicated people work together in trust and harmony—and with a sense of joy. Individuals in that group experience deep community and find that they connect with the deep yearnings and hungers of their lives. They find meanings and begin to articulate those meanings and values from their lived experience. So find a small group. It may be the church board or council, an intentional ministry group, or a selection group. You do not need to radically revamp the organizational chart. Just start with an existing group.

Find ways to help each group tell its story about the power of a lived experience. You can be sure that the dynamics of that story will affect other groups in the organization. Story will beget story, and so it grows until the whole church begins to change its character. Persons selected via an intentional discernment process—who have engaged in discernment themselves—will lead in a new way once they begin to function in a leadership capacity.

In this book we have tried to do just that by citing stories of biblical selectees and relaying the stories of living faith communities. We trust that this combined witness will resound to the glory of God and to the good of our beloved churches! Amen.

NOTES

CHAPTER 1

1. Mary Benet McKinney, *Sharing Wisdom: A Process for Group Decision Making* (Allen, Tex.: Tabor Publishing, 1987), 13.
2. Richard A Busch, "A Strange Silence," *The Christian Century*, March 22-29, 1995): 316-17.
3. Margaret Wheatley, *Leadership and the New Science: Learning about Organization from an Orderly Universe* (San Francisco: Barrett-Koehler Publishers, 1992), 20, 52.
4. Charlotte Shelton, *Quantum Leaps: Seven Skills for Workplace ReCreation* (Boston: Butterworth-Heinemann, 1999), 76.

CHAPTER 2

1. Craig Dykstra, *Growing in the Life of Faith* (Louisville, Ky.: Geneva Press, 1999), 69-70.
2. Danny E. Morris and Charles M. Olsen, *Discerning God's Will Together* (Nashville, Tenn.: Upper Room Books, 1997), 66 [in 4th and later printings, p. 78].
3. The Acts and Proceedings of the 194th Regular Session of the General Synod (New York: Reformed Church in America), 2000.
4. Morris and Olsen, *Discerning God's Will*, 74 [in 4th and later printings, p. 88].
5. Dietrich Bonhoeffer, *Life Together* (New York, Harper and Row, 1954), 26.

CHAPTER 3

1. Charles M. Olsen, *Transforming Church Boards into Communities of Spiritual Leaders* (Bethesda, Md.: The Alban Institute, 1995), 64.

2. Wheatley, *Leadership and the New Science*, 18-19.
3. Walter Wink, "The Spirits of Institutions," in *The Hidden Spirit: Discovering the Spirituality of Institutions,* ed. James F. Cobble Jr. and Charles M. Elliott (Matthews, N.C.: Christian Ministry Resources, 1999), 18.
4. Jessica Powers, "The Second Giving," in *Selected Poetry of Jessica Powers* (Washington, D.C.: ICS Publications, 1991), 133.

CHAPTER 6

1. Wheatley, *Leadership and the New Science*, 94.
2. Anne E. Carr, *Transforming Grace: Christian Tradition and Women's Experience* (San Francisco: Harper & Row, Publishers, 1988), 42.
3. Bonhoeffer, *Life Together*, 26.
4. John Cassian, The *Conferences,* trans. Boniface Ramsey (New York: Newman Press, 1997), 62.
5. *Ibid.*

CHAPTER 8

1. Denominations included in the survey: Christian Church (Disciples of Christ); Church of the Brethren; Church of the Nazarene; Episcopal Church; The Evangelical Covenant Church; The Evangelical Lutheran Church in America; Lutheran Church, Missouri Synod; Mennonite Church; Moravian Church in America; Presbyterian Church (U.S.A.); Society of Friends (Quakers); United Church of Christ; The United Methodist Church.
2. Austin Flannery, ed., *Vatican Council II: The Conciliar and Post Conciliar Documents,* rev. ed. (Northport, N.Y.: Costello Publishing Co., 1988).
3. *Book of Order,* Part II of The Constitution of the Presbyterian Church (U.S.A.) (Louisville, Ky.: The Office of the General

Assembly, 1997), G-1.01.

4. Arlin Rothauge, *Sizing Up a Congregation for New Member Ministry* (New York: The Episcopal Church Center).

5. Johannes Metz, *Followers of Christ: The Religious Life and the Church* (London: Burns and Oates, 1978), 12.

RESOURCES

Bass, Dorothy, ed. *Practicing Our Faith*. San Francisco: Jossey-Bass, 1997.

Bonhoeffer, Dietrich. *Life Together*. New York: Harper & Row, 1954.

Brueggemann, Walter. *Gathering the Church in the Spirit*. Decatur, Ga.: CTS Press, 1995.

Busch, Richard A. "A Strange Silence," *The Christian Century* (March 22-29, 1995): 316-17.

Callahan, Kennon L. *Effective Church Leadership*. San Francisco: HarperSanFrancisco, 1990.

Carr, Anne E. *Transforming Grace: Christian Tradition and Women's Experience*. San Francisco: Harper & Row, Publishers, 1988.

Cassian, John. *The Conferences*. Trans. Boniface Ramsey. New York: Newman Press, 1997.

Center for Pastoral Life and Ministry. *New Wine: The Kansas City Formation for Ministry Program*. Mahwah, N.J.: Paulist Press, 1995.

Duger, Sharon L. Pamela J. Lardear, and Garrie F. Stevens. *Seeking and Doing God's Will: Discernment for the Community of Faith*. Nashville, Tenn.: Discipleship Resources, 1998.

Dykstra, Craig. *Growing in the Life of Faith.* Louisville, Ky.: Geneva Press, 1999.

Farnham, Suzanne G. et al., *Listening Hearts: Discerning Call in Community.* Harrisburg, Pa.: Morehouse Publishing, 1991.

Hahn, Celia Allison. *Uncovering Your Church's Hidden Spirit.* Bethesda, Md.: The Alban Institute, 2001.

Heifetz, Ronald A. *Leadership Without Easy Answers.* Cambridge, Mass.: Harvard University Press, 1994.

Johnson, Luke Timothy. *Scripture and Discernment: Decision Making in the Church.* Nashville, Tenn.: Abingdon Press, 1996.

Keirsey, David and Marilyn Bates. *Please Understand Me: Character and Temperament Types.* Del Mar, Calif.: Prometheus Nemesis Books, 1978.

McKinney, Mary Benet. *Sharing Wisdom: A Process for Group Decision Making.* Allen, Tex.: Tabor Publishing, 1987.

Mead, Loren B. *The Once and Future Church.* Bethesda, Md.: The Alban Institute, 1991.

Metz, Johannes B. *Followers of Christ: The Religious Life and the Church.* London: Burns and Oates, 1978.

Miller, Art, Jr. and William Hendricks. *Why You Can't Be Whatever You Want to Be.* Grand Rapids, Mich.: Zondervan, 2000.

Morris, Danny E. and Charles M. Olsen. *Discerning God's Will Together: A Spiritual Practice for the Church*. Nashville, Tenn.: Upper Room Books, 1997.

Morseth, Ellen. *Call to Leadership: Transforming the Local Church*. Franklin, Wis.: Sheed & Ward, 1995.

————. *Ritual and the Arts in Spiritual Discernment*. Kansas City, Mo.: Worshipful-Work, 1999.

Olsen, Charles M. *Transforming Church Boards into Communities of Spiritual Leaders*. Bethesda, Md.: The Alban Institute, 1995.

Powers, Jessica. *Selected Poetry of Jessica Powers*. Ed. Regina Siegfried and Robert F. Morneau. Washington, D.C.: ICS Publications, 1991.

Rohr, Richard and Andreas Ebert. *Discovering the Enneagram*. New York: The Crossroad Publishing Company, 1992.

Rothauge, Arlin J. *Sizing Up a Congregation for New Member Ministry*. New York: The Episcopal Church Center (815 Second Avenue, New York, NY 10017).

Senge, Peter M. *The Fifth Discipline: Mastering the Five Practices of the Learning Organization*. New York: Doubleday, 1990.

Senge, Peter M. et al. *The Dance of Change*. New York: Doubleday, 1999.

Shelton, Charlotte. *Quantum Leaps: Seven Skills for Workplace ReCreation*. Boston: Butterworth-Heinemann, 1999.

Wagner, C. Peter. *Your Spiritual Gifts Can Help Your Church Grow.* Ventura, Calif.: Regal Books, 1997.

Ware, Corinne. *Discover Your Spiritual Type.* Bethesda, Md.: The Alban Institute, 1995.

Wheatley, Margaret J. *Leadership and the New Science: Learning about Organization from an Orderly Universe.* San Francisco: Berrett-Koehler Publishers, 1992.

Williams, Benjamin D. and Michael T. McKibben. *Oriented Leadership: Why All Christians Need It.* Wayne, N.J: Orthodox Christian Publications Center, 1994.

Wink, Walter. "The Spirit of Institutions," in *The Hidden Spirit, Discovering the Spirituality of Institutions,* James F. Cobble, Jr. and Charles M. Elliott, eds. Matthews, N.C.: Christian Ministry Resources, 1999.

INDEX OF
BIBLICAL WITNESSES

Charles M. Olsen is founder and Senior Mentor for Worshipful-Work Center for Transforming Religious Leadership in Kansas City. An ordained Presbyterian minister, he has served in local congregations as well as conference and national Presbyterian bodies. He received his M.Div. from Pittsburgh Theological Seminary.

Ellen Morseth is Staff Mentor for Worshipful-Work in Kansas City. A member of the Sisters of Charity, she is the author of *Ritual and the Arts in Spiritual Discernment* and *Call to Leadership: Transforming the Local Church.* She received her undergraduate degree from Mundelein College and her M.A. in pastoral counseling from Emmanuel College, Boston.